Today's Pastor
in
Tomorrow's World

Today's Pastor in Tomorrow's World

(REVISED EDITION)

by
Carnegie Samuel Calian

THE WESTMINSTER PRESS

PHILADELPHIA

BOOK DESIGN BY DOROTHY ALDEN SMITH

Published by The Westminster Press ®
Philadelphia, Pennsylvania

PRINTED IN THE UNITED STATES OF AMERICA
9 8 7 6 5 4 3 2 1

Library of Congress Cataloging in Publication Data

Calian, Carnegie Samuel.
  Today's pastor in tomorrow's world.

  Bibliography: p.
  Includes index.
  1. Pastoral theology. I. Title.
BV4011.C24 1982   253   82-7114
ISBN 0-664-24426-2   AACR2

To my students,
today's and tomorrow's pastors

Contents

(Continued)

Foreword

Not every seminary teacher is qualified to address the problems of being a pastor in a contemporary world. In an unusual way, Sam Calian has shown his understanding of both the practice of and the current thought and research about the practice of ministry. As a working theologian he has consistently endeavored to place various elements in or systems of our common life under theological and biblical scrutiny. Indeed, it is his own commitment to a working theology that has become the model of the pastor theologian. It is inconceivable to him that any person who carries responsibility for the spiritual nurture of people and a community can disclaim competence or interest in being a theologian. For that reason it becomes essential that the teachers of ministers be persons not just skilled in their disciplines but capable of theological address to the problems and issues of the contemporary world.

In this book Professor Calian presents persuasively the model for pastor as the grass-roots theologian. Building on the research of the Association of Theological Schools regarding readiness for the practice of ministry as defined by professionals and laypersons, he looks critically at the various models of pastor that have been proposed. He elucidates the lessons for the pastor learned from critical evaluation by laypersons, acknowledging how tough the job is. In a sensitive chapter he deals with the effect of women on the practice of pastoral grass-roots theology. In keeping with the theology of "the priesthood of all believers" he attempts to untangle and clarify the relationship of clergy and lay ministries. In a realistic assessment of the work possibilities, the author explores other possible channels of the ministry/priestly vocation at a time when employment as pastors seems more hazardous. Finally, he puts in a single chapter the theme of the book by spelling out the nature of a reshaped pastoral ministry and, by implication, of education for that reshaped task.

This book is an example of a working theology and as such should and will be used widely by students preparing for either clergy or lay leadership in congregations. It can be read with profit by all teachers, in whatever field, who are helping to prepare persons for the church's ministries. Most of all, in my judgment, this book can be of major assistance to practicing ministers who are engaged in critical examination of what they do week by week. For those men and women this will not be a disillusioning book but one that will help them to see their task clearly and in perspective. The church is helped by a working theologian addressing the work and nature of the pastoral ministry as Sam Calian has done, and we are grateful to him.

JESSE H. ZIEGLER
Former Executive Director
The Association of Theological Schools
in the United States and Canada

Preface

My ordination to the professional Christian ministry took place nearly twenty-five years ago. Throughout the years that followed, I have been especially aware of the importance of leadership within the church. This book is addressed to laity, clergy, and seminarians in our common quest to study and perhaps redirect our leadership to bring about more effectively our Christian mission in the future. The discussion contained in these pages is a summons to analyze realistically options and styles of ministry.

My own parish experience and teaching ministry have provided numerous contacts with the church at all levels of its life. These experiences are brought to the book, as well as readings and conversations with persons within and outside the church. Also, my travels in the United States and abroad have provided a wide variety of exposure to the Christian church. My reflections and outlook have not taken their final shape with the writing of this book; the dynamics of ministry will continue to challenge my thinking beyond the pages of this study. Indeed, the dynamics of ministry as they have changed even in the few years since the first edition of this book have caused me to make significant revisions in this new edition. While I have always believed in the ordination of women and their full participation in the life and leadership of the church, important changes in the social and religious scenes have required a substantial rewriting of parts of Chapter 3, now titled "Women and Men in Ministry." Changes and corrections also have been made in the other chapters of the book.

I owe a special debt to my clergy colleagues who have taught me much through the years, especially my students.

This book is written in an ecumenical spirit, reflecting the environment in which I have been teaching for nearly two decades. I am indebted to the faculties at Wartburg Theological Seminary (American Lutheran), Aquinas Institute of Theology (Catholic, Dominican Order), and the University of Dubuque Theological Seminary (United Presbyterian) for their partnership and stimulation. My experiences in team teaching with these faculty members have especially widened my scope and understanding of ministry. My new colleagues at Pittsburgh Theological Seminary have also in a short time contributed to my understanding of ministry.

Countless retreats, conferences, young pastor schools, and other gatherings with clergy and laity have been a major source of information and inspiration. My brief teaching visits at Lutheran Theological Seminary in Philadelphia, Princeton Theological Seminary, and Fuller Theological Seminary have also widened my exposure to pastors and seminarians and their concerns. The Council of Theological Seminaries of The United Presbyterian Church U.S.A. has also contributed to my perspective on the Reformed understanding of ministry. The Association of Theological Schools has provided opportunities for encountering the complexities of theological education in a wide spectrum of schools.

To my long-standing friends, both clergy and laity, I express my indebtedness and gratitude for their friendship, candor, and encouragement through the years. A world without friends would indeed be a tragedy.

This list of acknowledgments must include an enthusiastic appreciation to the trustees, administration, faculty, and students of Juniata College, where I have served as the first occupant of the J. Omar Good Visiting Distinguished Professorship of Evangelical Christianity. Two years on Juniata's campus provided satisfying and memorable experiences for my entire family.

My grateful appreciation to Peg Saunders, Debbie Lynn, and Linda Smith for typing the manuscript, to Priscilla Boyd for preparing the index, to Ralph Church and my wife, Doris, for helpful editorial comments, to Lillian Staiger and Denise Blaisdell for their resourceful assistance in the library, and to William H. Gentz, then editor of Hawthorn Books, whose support made the original edition of this book a reality. My appreciation to the editors and publisher of The Westminster Press for their encouragement to have a new and revised edition of this book. Full responsibility for the contents of this book is mine alone.

1

The Situation Today

"Can the laity expect greatness from the clergy?" An active layperson confronted me with that question one day. The layperson, a successful businessman, had both a son and a son-in-law in the ministry. He was raising the question out of genuine concern for the church and its impact upon the public.

The discussion within the pages of this book is an examination of that question—an inquiry that encompasses the present as well as the future. The layman who raised the question was not asking it out of a vacuum. He had some particular expectation of the clergy—perhaps an expectation that was not being fulfilled. What was his idea of greatness? Did he want parish pastors to be Nobel Prize winners? Did he want today's clergy to emulate the great pastors of the past? Individuals do have their pastoral heroes. Or was he simply trying to tell me, a seminary professor responsible for the training of tomorrow's clergy, something of his dissatisfaction with the present practice of ministry? All of these half-formulated thoughts and questions flashed through my mind as I listened for clues during the remainder of our conversation.

Fulfilling the Laity's Expectations

Knowing and fulfilling the expectations of the laity is a great concern for pastors and theological educators. In a decade of declining membership, retrenchment, and pastoral surpluses, it is questionable whether these expectations are even recognized. The Association of Theological Schools in the United States and Canada has been engaged in an assessment report determining what it is that the laity and the clergy expect in ministry. The Association includes Protestant, Orthodox, Catholic, and Jewish accredited theological institutions, representing constituents in forty-seven ecclesiastical organizations. The report is entitled *Readiness for Ministry.*[1] The respondents to the scientific survey were equally divided among laity and clergy. The latter group consisted of seminary professors, clergy active in the field, denominational leaders, and senior seminary students. The respondents, numbering more than two thousand, indicated a large measure of consensus among clergy and laity in their expectations for fledgling clergy beginning their ministry. The findings of the study were:

1. The most significant characteristic or criterion that people across denominational lines are seeking in their young clergy is "service without regard for personal acclaim." This "describes an individual who is able to accept personal limitations and, believing the Gospel, is able to serve without concern for public recognition."
2. People want a pastor who shows personal integrity. This is interpreted as "one who is able to honor commitments by carrying out promises despite all pressures to compromise."
3. People desire an exemplary individual in their pas-

tor. Such an individual is described as "one whose personal belief in the Gospel manifests itself in generosity, and in general, a Christian example that people in the community can respect."

4. Listed fourth among expectations are particular pastoral skills. These involve "the responsible functioning of one who shows competence and responsibility by completing tasks, by being able to handle differences of opinions and who senses the need to continue to grow in pastoral skills."

5. People want a minister who is a leader in community building. This implies a pastor who "will build a strong sense of community within a congregation. It includes taking time to know parishioners well and developing a sense of trust and confidence between pastor and parish."

6. People want a pastor who can be described as a perceptive counselor, "as one who reaches out to persons under stress with a perception, sensitivity, and warmth that is freeing and supportive."

7. People would like in their pastor a theologian and thinker. For the respondents this characterized "a person's basic intelligence as demonstrated in communication." This concern involves the need to sharpen an already keen intelligence with further theological study and attention to clarity of thought and expression.

8. People look for a pastor "who is able to handle stressful situations by remaining calm under pressure while continuing to affirm persons."

9. People want a pastor "who is able to acknowledge limitations and mistakes and recognize the need for continued growth and learning."

On the negative side of the ledger, the report indicates that people do not want a pastor who practices a self-serving ministry—one "who avoids intimacy and people with a critical, demeaning, and insensitive attitude." Furthermore, they reject clergy who are involved in "illicit sexual relationships and other self-indulgent actions that irritate, shock, or offend." People are also disappointed in pastors who show "emotional immaturity and actions that demonstrate immaturity, insecurity, and insensitivity when buffeted by the demands and pressures of the profession."

In short, the report highlights that clergy and laity together want their ministers to clearly affirm and live the gospel they have been called to proclaim. The laity want to share in ministry with clergy who both know God and acknowledge their human limitations. It might appear from this list that the laity are searching for a superhuman individual as their pastor. In actuality, the characteristics of an ideal pastor should be seen as guidelines—criteria that those involved in professional ministry ought to bear in mind constantly. As the report rightly suggests, God's people "are looking for one who is able to face all human limitations and yet be a vehicle of God's witness and service in the world of need. It is clear that ministry lies at the center of people's expectations. It is not intellect or any given skill that people are looking for in ministers. Rather, it is the integration of a good mind, counseling skills, preaching ability, and all the rest they want, incarnate in a person who seeks to minister to *them* as persons." Perhaps this is a description of the greatness that the businessman was hoping to find. Or maybe the report only underlines the suspicion of many that the ideal pastor exists only in speculation and that greatness in ministry is an illusive goal as we face the realities and limitations before us. Perhaps greatness should not even be a goal.

The United Presbyterian Church, like other denominations, has been losing members during the last decade. The denomination wants to know why. What expectations do the laity have of the church and the professional clergy? The denomination conducted a survey on "Church Membership Trends," which reported to the church's General Assembly.[2] The survey showed that many of the popular theories for explaining membership losses were ill-founded. For instance, the attempts to explain membership losses in the churches by (1) increased leisure time, (2) use and reliance upon mass media, (3) influence of science, (4) standard of living, and (5) competition of secular or volunteer organizations cannot be supported, since each of these factors was already present and increasing in the 1940s and 1950s as well as in the 1960s.

The survey did indicate that loss of membership was more apt to be caused by the dropping birthrate and a change in values, especially among young people. Young people tend to think out religious and moral questions for themselves, with less reliance on churchly authority. The church is not in the center of their value orientation.

Another factor contributing to loss of membership is the inability to handle conflict situations in the church. Such conflicts often rise in relation to social action issues, as seen in the disagreement over the disbursement of United Presbyterian funds in 1971 for the defense fund for Angela Davis. Resolving the conflict following this social action either strengthened or lost the leadership in many local situations. It appears that church leadership has not been adequately trained to deal with conflict situations, thus causing members to be disenchanted during the period of conflict.

The fact that inflated membership rolls are being trimmed of inactive members has been another but inadequate explanation for decline, as is the often-heard stipulation that the lack of theological conservatism and neglect of the Bible may be the reason for loss of membership. The survey indicated that the rise or fall of membership apparently depends far more on the strength, clarity, warmth, and enthusiasm of the church leadership and program than on its theological viewpoint. It is this accent on leadership in the report that deserves further attention in our discussion.

The membership report indicated strongly that churches that are growing have vital pastoral leadership. Members have expressed great satisfaction with pastors who show competence in preaching, pastoral calling, communicating warmth and sensitivity to members' needs, pastoral prayers, and ability to generate enthusiasm and spiritual authenticity. "Members of growing congregations perceive their pastors as having more responsibility for church growth and as more able to handle conflict positively and to develop a spirit of unity in the congregation."[3] In short, the pastor in a growing church knows how to develop teamwork within the membership of the church.

The survey illustrates that the caliber of leadership is a far more determinative factor to church growth than the question of liberal or conservative positions, social action, or purely personal-individual religious experience and expression. This does not imply that the theology or conviction of the leader or congregation is of no consequence. "Rather, it is to say that the conviction, enthusiasm, warmth, and competence with which the Christian faith and life is shared communicates more effectively."[4] One of the concluding remarks of the report is that despite the dangers of "clericalism," it is absolutely necessary to upgrade the quality of professional leadership if the churches are to grow and the expectations of the laity are to be met.

To that end, the laity will expect from the ordained ministry in the future greater "(1) clarity, strength and persuasiveness of Christian conviction and commitment; (2) good preaching and the ability to design and lead meaningful worship; (3) conviction of and commitment to pastoral calling as integral to Christian ministry and pastoral care; (4) deep sensitivity to the needs of people individually and in groups; (5) concern for, dedication to, and skill in working for congregational development and growth as a part of faithfulness, for the nurture and retention of members who show signs of slackening commitment, for the motivation and training of laypersons to work for church growth; (6) capacity to generate enthusiasm in other people, personal warmth, competence, spiritual authenticity; (7) ability to encourage and generate a spirit of unity in a congregation; and (8) organizational development and conflict management skills."

Will the fulfillment and performance of the above list of expectations point the clergy in the direction of greatness? And is the fulfillment of these expectations within the realm of possibility? To what extent are these expectations being met in the current models of ministry?

Current Models of Ministry: An Appraisal

There are at least eight distinguishable styles of ministry in vogue today. I have labeled them for convenience in our discussion as the following: (1) the servant-shepherd, (2) the politician-prophet, (3) the preacher-teacher, (4) the evangelist-charismatic, (5) the pragmatist-promoter, (6) the manager-enabler, (7) the liturgist-celebrant, and (8) specialized ministries such as hospital chaplaincy and marriage counseling. I believe that most other distinguishable models of ministry can be included within these categories.

How are these current styles of ministry faring in today's marketplace? Beginning with the *servant-shepherd* model, we have seen in our earlier discussion that this particular style meets with very favorable expectation from a large number of the laity. This model of ministry seeks to serve "without acclaim," and attempts to minister with sensitivity to the needs of people individually and in groups. This model oscillates between the selfless servant-pastor and the pastor who serves as the loving elder and parent to the congregation. Many pastors see themselves practicing this style of ministry. At least, this is how they would like to be perceived by the parish. This model is based upon Jesus as the suffering servant. From the 1950s to the early 1970s the servant theology of ministry dominated the curriculum of most theological seminaries. There is no doubt that the practice of this model of ministry is deeply satisfying.

Take, for instance, the reflections of Msgr. Vincent A. Yzermans, former editor of *Our Sunday Visitor*, a national Roman Catholic weekly. His parish was in Sauk Centre, Minnesota. He lived there six years and was the proud and happy pastor of 115 families, including 761 persons. It was a rural parish—a small, closely knit group of persons who were lovers of farm and family. The parish was proud of its solid Catholic German ethnicity and the rich black soil among the rolling hills of central Minnesota. Listen to his remarks on those parish days—as the servant-shepherd of the flock:

> During the six years I had been pastor there I came to know and deeply love these good people of God. I had baptized 74 children, witnessed 32 marriages, laid to rest in God's holy acre 24 members of the parish. As statistics go, minimal; as love goes, infinite . . . *this* pastor left a bit of his heart in *that* parish. He also stamped his brand on that parish, for better or worse. I suppose that is the best expression, after all. As husband and wife, so pastor and parish, take each other "for better or worse." They might not remember your name, but in years to come they will say, "We once had a pastor who . . ." When all is said and done, that is the best tribute one can and should expect. It recognizes a pastor, any pastor, for what he is, or should be—a man of God.[5]

I read Msgr. Yzermans' reflections several times and was moved with the simplicity of his account. There are clergy in every tradition who could echo these sentiments. There are also clergy who would seriously question this servant-shepherd model as being unrealistic. Some pastors are guilt-ridden by their inability to emulate this model, while others feel it is an impossible model, given the realities of living with any parish. Msgr. Yzermans readily admits in his article that the servant-shepherd model is less than idyllic. The pastor must restrain personal emotions on occasion, difficult as that may be. He is called upon to be parent and elder to all without being intimate to any. When honest with himself, Msgr. Yzermans confesses that at times he has been curt and impatient, especially when people call during the dinner hour. His own shortcomings on sermon preparations and visits to parishioners he blames on the time he stole for some relaxation and personal enjoyment. Protestant readers might conclude at this point that the servant-shepherd model might be a possibility for celibates; it certainly does not seem to be a viable option for clergy with families.

Actually, the servant-shepherd model should include all persons who consider themselves among the people of God. In other words, this model is not exclusively limited to the professional clergy. The servant-shepherd model applies to the entire *laos*— the people of God. Each member of the ecclesiastical household must take seriously the implications of the priesthood of all believers. We have *all* been baptized into a common priesthood. We are all disciples. There are no first- and second-class Christians. We are called upon to serve and to celebrate a common ministry. Our Christian vocation is to be servants and shepherds to each other. We are a household of believers whose status before God is one of serving and shepherding for specific tasks. I think it is a poor theology that nurtures and conditions church people to expect a core of persons to be "selfless servants" and "shepherds" while the remainder of the flock does its own thing—playing Christian when it is convenient.

The priesthood of *all* believers is a reminder to us all that our time, talent, and resources are on loan to us from God. Each of us is called into a priestly vocation—from God's standpoint we are a body of believers, not a divided church of clergy and laity. Any kind of laicism or clericalism in the church is detrimental to the life and health of the Christian fellowship. There is nothing theologically wrong with the servant-shepherd model, only the tendency to limit its de facto application to the clergy. We must rediscover this model as a goal of discipleship for all believers.

> Jesus called them to him and said, "You know that in the world the recognized rulers lord it over their subjects, and their great men make them feel the weight of authority. That is not the way with you; among you, whoever wants to be great must be your servant, and whoever wants to be first must be the willing slave of all. For even the Son of Man did not come to be served but to serve, and to give up his life as a ransom for many." (Mark 10:42–45, NEB)

It is only when pastor and people see themselves as belonging to a common ministry that we can hope realistically for servanthood and shepherding to succeed in the parish. Without this partnership, the priesthood of all believers is denied an opportunity to become actual reality in the parish.

The *politician-prophet* model of the pastor has a lower profile today than it did in the 1960s when it was closely associated with the civil rights movement and the war in Vietnam. Many pastors are still licking their wounds and memories from those years, while others have dropped out of the parish ministry.[6] This particular style of ministry tends to be seen more often among younger clergy, celibate priests (and sisters), ethnic-oriented clergy, and women ministers.

Many examples of the period stand out in our memories: Philip and Daniel Berrigan, whose cause placed them on the front cover of *Time* magazine. I wonder if the Berrigans are an example of the greatness sought by that business layman? There was the significant ministry and leadership of Martin Luther King, Jr., whose commitment cost him his life. William Sloan Coffin, Jr., and Malcolm Boyd also received national notoriety for their positions on social issues of the day. In Chicago's South Side, the Rev. John Fry, who was then serving at the First Presbyterian Church, made headlines for his controversial ministry with a militant street gang (the Blackstone Rangers). His ministry brought him in opposition to the police and local authorities. Although he was ultimately vindicated, Fry's involvement and subsequent slander indicated the price to be paid in following a politician-prophet model of ministry.

In South America, there was the case of Father Enrique Pereira Neto, the twenty-six-year-old chaplain of the Catholic Student Youth who was kidnapped and tortured before being killed for his opposition to Brazilian government policies. The courageous stand of Brazil's Archbishop Dom Helder Câmara in his struggle for political justice and freedom is well known throughout the international ecumenical community. The liberation theology from Latin America is also based upon the politician-prophet model of ministry.

There is no question that the politician-prophet style of ministry must continue if the church is to be a conscience raiser in society. Those who follow this model take a calculated risk, as did the Rev. John Witherspoon in the founding of our nation. John Witherspoon, a Presbyterian pastor, was the only minister to sign the Declaration of Independence. He was for many years a pastor in Scotland and the United States, as well as the first president of the College of New Jersey (later to become Princeton University), and a member of Congress. Is Witherspoon an example of the greatness in ministry that we seek in tomorrow's clergy?

It is my belief that the politician-prophet model of ministry must be integrated into the clergy's total theological understanding of the people of God. That is to say, the politician-prophet model calls primarily for working with the congregation in a frank and open manner. The politician-prophet style in the parish can best be implemented not from the pulpit or from the cloakroom, but out in the open on a common footing with the congregation. The pastor must stand among the people in the middle, like the hub of a wheel, and allow the people to span out and blanket the community as change agents. Often pastors in the name of leadership have taken too prominent a role, only to be put down; others have operated in the rear from some back room, causing people to feel that they have been manipulated. The pastor who leads from the middle integrates the politician-prophet style into total ministry with the *laos*. The pastor who operates from the middle is mindful of the theological power derived from the doctrine of the priesthood of all believers.

The *preacher-teacher* model has had long historic roots back to apostolic times. The Reformation reinforced this style, as witnessed in the lives of Martin Luther, John Calvin, Theodore Beza, John Knox, and others. There was a time in recent years when preaching was considered passé, but today more attention is given to homiletics in the training of all seminarians. The pulpit as the teaching desk continues as a very significant symbol within the life of the church. It is true that the quality of preaching varies considerably from parish to parish, depending upon the time invested, the talents of the preacher, and previous training.

It may seem too harsh a judgment to make, but it has been my observation in both small and large congregations that the laity on the whole are suffering from respectful boredom with most of today's preaching. If your experience is more promising, you are among the fortunate exceptions. We need to face the reality that most pulpit communication is not reaching its goal. The tragedy is that pastor and people have intentionally built a wall of illusion in this area based upon sweet platitudes. The reality is that only minimal attention is given to the listening process. Most congregations adjust their expectations in this area as they turn to the other gifts and talents found in their pastor. Yet each time churches seek a new pastor, expectations rise again for a preacher-teacher style of ministry, only to adjust downward again, showing appreciation for the other qualities and skills in their pastor.

Frankly, I do not believe that seminaries can produce "princes in the pulpit." Training can certainly help to bring out what talent is latently there. But the reality is that the preacher-teacher model may be at one and the same time every seminarian's wish and ultimate source of frustration. To take account of this fact is *not* to say that every pastor should stop aspiring to preach and teach. Certainly not! Rather, it is to say that one's pastoral model should not be built solely upon this style of ministry to the neglect of other aspects of ministry. The preacher-teacher model, when integrated with other styles, can be a very satisfying aspect of one's total ministry.

Pastors in a community who have come to this realization can greatly enrich the spiritual diet of their parishioners by establishing a regular preaching schedule of exchanges within the local community. Most pulpit exchanges today are limited to the summer months and during the week of Christian Unity. A more frequent exchange program will give the laity variety and enable the pastor to prepare fewer and, it is hoped, more effective sermons that can be preached more than once. It is my suspicion that to have a new sermon theme (as most homiletic courses seem to assume) every week is too demanding. It is one reason why our preaching is spotty and the laity bored. To preach one good sermon several times in a given community would enable each pastor to develop more careful sermons, which would benefit more persons within the larger community. The preacher-teacher model (executed in some kind of regular rotation basis in the future) would maximize the pastor's limited time and resources and could more effectively approximate the expectations of the laity who are seeking more meaningful preaching and teaching.

Of course, larger churches with a pastor who specializes in preaching may have no need for such a program. However, the majority of churches across the country are under the leadership of a single pastor. The rotation program would be ideally suited for these parishes. Local ministeriums will become alive overnight where the pastors are engaged in meaningful cooperation of this kind throughout the year. Such a ministry can actually be to the mutual interest and edification of God's people in an entire locality.

In a decade of declining church membership, the *evangelist-charismatic* model of ministry is receiving more attention today. This particular style of ministry, often associated with Billy Graham on the grand scale, is practiced at the grass roots on a more personal and intimate basis by pastors who have an active concern to introduce persons to Jesus Christ and to see the church as the fellowship of forgiven sinners.

The Rev. Robert S. Lutz, formerly pastor of the Corona Presbyterian Church in Denver, Colorado, is a good example of a pastor who follows this style of ministry. For him, there is nothing more exciting than leading another person to Christ. The Corona church is located in a changing community of persons in the middle and the lower economic strata, made up of blacks, Egyptians, Koreans, and members of several other minority groups. Lutz, an evangelical pastor for thirty-eight years, was able to attract this diverse community of persons to his church with his evangelist-charismatic style of ministry. Lutz was also associated with a coffeehouse group that called itself "The Holy Ghost Repair Service." On the National Day of Humiliation, Fasting, and Prayer in May 1974 more than three hundred members of the coffeehouse group came to pray. " 'Some of these long-haired young people believe in speaking in tongues,' says Lutz. 'I don't, but I just tell them that I love Jesus, they love Jesus, so let's get on with it. And we do.' "[7]

The evangelist-charismatic style of ministry provides the parish ministry with a dimension of enthusiasm and warmth often lost in a church afraid to express its emotions and confront directly the meaning of salvation and the Holy Spirit's activity in changing lives. On the other hand, there are limitations to this model in its understanding of evangelism and charismatic awakening among the people of God. This style of ministry ought to include consciously a dimension of "Socratic evangelism" as well.[8] The Socratic evangelist is willing to listen as well as to save. Such ministry can then speak, without seeming naive, of today's imperfect world in which persons find themselves. *Christianity Today*, in an editorial entitled "Developing a Climate for Evangelism," warned its readers that "evangelicals need to concede that they often have very little idea of what today's unbeliever is thinking and where the great gaps in his Christian knowledge lie."[9] The pastor who is practicing an evangelist-charismatic style of ministry should seriously heed the editorial. Pastors who include a Socratic dimension in their practice of ministry are willing to have their own absolutes examined and scrutinized by another party. The confidence of the pastor in such a dialogue is squarely placed in the Holy Spirit to prevail throughout the encounter. This style of ministry is open to the possibility that the pastor does not comprehend the whole truth, but witnesses to the truth of the gospel limited by a particular time and space. Hence such practice of ministry does not become dated; it is ever fresh to the winds of the Spirit.

The *pragmatist-promoter* model of ministry has great appeal out of necessity. We live in a society of pragmatism and promotions. Ours is a business culture that is both functionally and materially oriented.[10] Every pastor I know is by necessity a pragmatist and a promoter. The situation is true of the laity as well. In such a climate, a "great pastor" is seen as one whose leadership has helped to build a new sanctuary or church school plant and whose effective action in decision-making has placed the church in a strong financial and social position in the community. Perhaps the best-known and most respected exponent of this pragmatist-promoter style of ministry is Norman Vincent Peale, whose supporters and critics are countless. Whatever else might be said of Peale, we must agree that he understands the success motivations of our business culture. In Garden Grove, California, there is the ministry of Robert H. Schuller, whose Crystal Cathedral, with its drive-in features, is also nationally known. Among predominantly black churchgoers there is the phenomenal rise in the ministry of Frederick Eikerenkoetter, better known to his followers as Reverend Ike. Both Schuller and Ike have organizations to implement further their understanding of ministry. Schuller conducts an Institute for Successful Church Life, which one supporter described as "the most thrilling experience since I accepted Jesus Christ." Schuller's basic emphases are (1) possibility thinking (similar in approach to Peale's positive thinking),

(2) stress upon pastoral leadership as the key, (3) outstanding surroundings and furnishings to impress the unchurched, (4) a noncontroversial, always positive approach, (5) a good staff and educational program.[11] This approach has given Schuller a "success story" in churchmanship.

The example of Reverend Ike has also found an enthusiastic response from his followers. Reverend Ike's basic approach to those striving for social upward mobility is to articulate the success philosophy of the upper middle class from his organizational headquarters based in Brookline, Massachusetts, and known as the United Christian Evangelist Association. Reverend Ike tells his followers that "people can love the Lord a lot better when they have money to pay their bills and meet their needs. . . . I think it is the lack of money, not the love of money, which is the root of all evil. . . . There is no man who is so rich or so poor that he is not interested in health, happiness, love, success, and prosperity, which is what I am all about."[12] There is nothing apologetic in the pragmatist-promoter style of ministry practiced by each of these men.

All pastors need to admit that each of us would like to experience a measure of success in our ministry. How to realize our ambition has often left us frustrated and guilt-ridden. It is not difficult to debunk Peale, Schuller, and Ike on theological and biblical grounds—their style of ministry is certainly not the suffering servant example of Jesus, whose own ministry led to crucifixion. Yet we can no more escape the pragmatist-promoter dimension within our ministry than we can escape from our business culture. The question that faces each of us is: To what extent do we want the ministry in our churches to pay the price of being counter-culture, to carry a cross in the name of Jesus—the Suffering Servant? This question poses a tension that must be openly discussed by every congregation that is seeking biblical and theological direction for its witness. Pastors who think they are above our culture's standards of success are kidding themselves; the laity are looking for pastors who will be successful.[13] As the people of God, we must ask ourselves if our expectations are biblical; do they need to be renegotiated in the light of Christ? It is hoped that new expectations will emerge in the future that will place limits upon the pragmatist-promoter style of ministry guided by biblical and theological norms rooted in sound Christology.

Today's pastor is increasingly captive to the *manager-enabler* model of ministry. This style sees the minister as the manager or pastor-director who participates within the congregation as an enabler. Mission through management and wise planning is the key. The framework views the pastor as the hired executive of the parish, employed to give a sense of direction to the whole planning process. Hence pastors are following the example of corporation executives and mastering such terms as management by objectives, goal-setting, priority determination, evaluation, and support systems. I suspect tht Jesus would find such terminology strange. Life is said to be much more complicated today than it was during the world of Jesus, but is it really? Have the essential aspects of living changed? Is the manager-enabler the type of pastor who will reach greatness and bring the church to a higher vision? A whole new corps of church consultants has emerged, promising to bring pastors and people to a new threshold of service through carefully planned management and forecasting. The pastor operating as a professional manager views organizational power in terms of generating growth in others. The pastor believes this style of ministry will enable individuals in the parish to grow and assume responsibility. The end result will be a more efficient church, greater involvement, and ownership of the enterprise by the people.

Organizing and planning are certainly essential aspects

of ministry. An experienced pastor once shared with me that "the minister cannot be a good evangelist without first being a good organizer." The manager-enabler style of minister is necessary, but it is no panacea for any congregation or pastor that has not sharply focused and defined theological goals. Management is a means; it does not help us to define our ends. As Peter Drucker, the management specialist, wisely observes: "Management is a tool to reach your own objectives. So my first question to a religious organization is always, 'What are you trying to accomplish?' And often I find that they are in a crisis of objectives, not of organization."[14] The pastor who primarily seeks to serve as the manager-enabler will not be able to help the congregation see beyond their crisis of objectives; the pastor's role is to provide theological guidelines in furthering the mission and vision of that congregation in their local community and beyond.

The manager-enabler model of ministry is tempted to dilute the biblical norms into a "theology of the feasible." What is feasible may in retrospect prove to be not only bad theology but serve as a definite barrier in that church's search for identity under God. The manager-enabler may have many persons working on several committees, but the end result may be nothing more than sheer confusion. Drucker tells us quite clearly that the "Church can be run with one-tenth of the committees they have without the slightest impairment of anything."[15] It is about time that the laity who understand our business culture so well stop their pastors and inform them of the limits of the manager-enabler style of ministry. What is applicable to corporate structures may not always be applied wisely to churches. Churches are more than businesses! I'm afraid that note has not been sounded clearly enough in recent years; as a result, unfortunately, the pastor-planner-manager-enabler has become the quintessence of today's ministry.

The *liturgist-celebrant* model of ministry has been a

traditional mainstay of pastors throughout the centuries. In more recent years congregations have witnessed innovations in this model. This has been true for Protestants as well as Catholics. The Eastern Orthodox clergy for the most part view the liturgist-celebrant as *the* model of their ministry. The format of Orthodox services has remained constant over the years. This style of ministry fulfills many important functions, the chief of which is to remind the people of God of the transcendent dimension of reality that is at the core of the Christian faith. Humankind's chief end is to worship and glorify God—to confess privately and publicly our stewardship and dependence upon the divine. The liturgist-celebrant leads us to the threshold of this truth each time we gather for thanksgiving and praise.

It would be an uplifting day in our churches if each pastor of whatever tradition took more seriously the celebrant role. There is a yearning in every congregation for a wider dimension of reality and a reminder that the pressures and strivings of the moment are fleeting from God's perspective of loving care. However, many pastors either have lost their sense of the transcendent or have not been adequately prepared to lead their parishioners into a meaningful worship experience. Individuals in each tradition at times feel that another tradition is doing a better job of liturgical celebration, but my observation has been that we are all in need of making worship experiences more meaningful. Dr. Leander E. Keck, dean of Yale Divinity School, believes that today's disarray of Christian worship is "a symptom of the loss of the Gospel, the demise of Christian theology, and a failure of nerve."[16] Pastors must give more attention to the liturgist-celebrant style of ministry. Perhaps greatness in the ministry lies with that pastor who can creatively quicken the imagination and thoughts of the congregation through worship of the eternal verities.

The final model of ministry practiced today includes the

various *specialized ministries* such as marriage counseling, hospital chaplaincy, and campus pastorates. Most of these specialized ministries today tend to be in counseling areas. There are also ad hoc specialities that pastors fulfill in a given community or on assignment for a church staff. In a time of financial crunch, many of the ad hoc specialities are terminated for budget-cutting purposes. Most denominations continue to view specialities as peripheral to the church's main task—the parish ministry. Specialization in ministry, contrary to specialization in medicine, is still not widely accepted.

It is my feeling that the future pastor will see greater specialization among the clergy. Ministry in the future will be practiced in a more sophisticated fashion than it has been in the past. Specialization will not be limited to staffs of large churches, but through creative cooperation pastors in smaller churches will take the opportunity to maximize their talents and educational skills to the benefit of the total community. Specialization in ministry takes cognizance of the fact that we live in a world of complex needs. A specialist is able to bring a dimension of authority to his particular area. Such authority is often missed by pastors who practice a general ministry. The future pastor will be faced increasingly with the tension between being a specialist (in terms of particular skills and competencies) and serving as a generalist within a local parish. It is the generalists in today's parish who are experiencing doubt about their effectiveness in ministry and see their authority eroding with the congregation. One of the purposes of this book is to assist this parish pastor in recovering confidence and effectiveness.

The sum total of these current models of ministry when integrated with each other presents a formidable image of the pastor. Is a successful packaging of all these aspects in one pastor what that business layman meant when he asked the question, "Can people expect greatness in their clergy?" Is his expectation realistic? What should the laity expect of their clergy? And also, what expectation should the clergy have of their laity? The fact that there are no immediate answers to these larger questions only emphasizes the unrest and searching within today's ranks of both clergy and laity. The questioning has brought a certain loss of confidence between each of the parties involved.

Overcoming the Loss of Confidence

Loss of confidence is a characteristic of our day. Clergy and laity are not exempt from this general malady. The crisis of leadership in organized religion accounts in part for the declining enthusiasm and falling membership witnessed in recent years. The phenomenon is ecumenically widespread, found among conservatives as well as liberals, Jews as well as Christians. The laity are eyeing their clergy with suspicion and mistrust. The clergy likewise are being very cautious in their relationships with the laity. No single explanation can unravel the causes of this loss of confidence and increasing disenchantment between clergy and laity. This condition is unfortunate and needs to be remedied. Whatever the specific causes—from petty personality differences to major disagreements over moral, social, and economic issues—a new strategy for credibility must be sought.

The future of our churches will depend upon responsible and responsive leadership. Our theological schools are preparing men and women to assume this leadership. Tomorrow's laity, concerned and better informed, will increasingly seek more meaningful partnership with this emerging leadership. Caught then between tomorrow's hopes and yesterday's traditions, the present voices from the pulpit and the pew are struggling to restore trust among themselves. Will they succeed? Will a common strategy of credibility emerge? Can a trusting climate reverse the trend of recent years? I believe it can. Let me suggest some guidelines through which the trust and confidence can be achieved between clergy and laity.

First, a public confession by clergy and laity of their mutual mistrust must be openly declared. Many will disclaim that mistrust exists, while others may be tempted to indulge in excessive counterproductive confessing. The purpose of confessing is to state candidly that each party has had misgivings about the wisdom and actions of the other. For instance, some laity may be convinced that the church is too important to be trusted to the clergy. Conversely, some clergy may feel that the laity are unworthy of the church. Allowing this underlying uneasiness to surface is a necessary part of the confessing process. It will indicate the extent or lack of trust existing between the parties. If trust is absent, then both sides must search diligently for a common platform of self-interest and trust-building. This is never easy to do, especially when each side feels threatened or manipulated. Yet someone with spiritual maturity must initiate the reconciling process if forgiveness and healing are to take place.

Second, the laity must overcome the temptation to crush the ecclesiastical leader every time a decision, act, or program runs contrary to expectations or vested interests. The laity often have been responsible for the frequent turnover of religious leadership at the local and national levels. Such radical shifts are detrimental for both clergy and laity and do not inspire confidence in either party. Both sides must remember that the test of good leadership includes taking an unpopular position if the integrity of the institution is to be maintained. Only in retrospect can such an action be determined as a wise or foolish decision.

Prophetic leadership demands and needs from the laity a measure of freedom to lead without having to turn each moment for approval. It is not easy for the laity to provide this psychic space; it must be earned. Once earned, it will be seen as a trusted bond and as achieving the necessary psychic space in which to operate.

Leadership, religious or otherwise, must make a periodic accounting of its trust. It is at this moment that responsible laity must carefully scrutinize their leader's record. To fail to do so is to invite trouble in the future. At the same time, laity must discipline themselves against hasty judgments in reaction to ecclesiastical decisions. Some distance and the benefit of prayerful reflection are required. Simply put, the laity must avoid ecclesiastical lynchings that might in retrospect be considered martyrdoms.

Third, prophetic religious leadership must have a clearly conceived program, otherwise it is headed for trouble. The loss of confidence in religious leadership is due in no small measure to prophets with shallow programs of action, which exhaust lay energy and generally contribute confusion to the genuine problems at hand.

Prophetic leadership should concentrate on education as well as action. This will help clarify the issues and provide adequate input from the membership. There are really no instant ways to enlightenment on the social ills of the day. It is a painfully slow process. The usual response to a crisis is no more than a first-aid approach that is largely forgotten a short time afterward. The prophet as educator must search with parishioners for the roots of these crises and thereby build a constructive solution for the future. Such a role is not glamorous, but the long-lasting consequences of educating might be more beneficial and renewing for society.

Fourth, both clergy and laity must acknowledge the existing tension between means and ends in applying one's faith to action. Concrete problems in contemporary society often have more than one means of solution, but there is sometimes a tendency to canonize one means over another. A limited means leads to a breakdown in communication. This becomes even more tragic when the ends are often held in common. The disparity among means explains why political parties exist in a democratic society, but members of religious organizations have a unique witness to make beyond these political groupings—namely, to show that means and ends are ultimately related. For the believer, means and ends must be mutually compatible, otherwise there is no significance to a religious and ethical frame of reference. It is precisely at this point that religious leadership needs to challenge and educate people to become a creative model within the larger society where means and ends are seriously wedded.

Fifth, religious clergy must more consciously share ownership of the leadership role with laity. This, of course, is already practiced in some instances, but for the most part clerical leadership dominates. The laity need to share more the administrative duties of the clergy, thus freeing the professional to attend to the primary theological task for which he or she was trained. Any viable strategy of credibility requires a greater portion of the clergy's time to be spent in the library preparing heart and mind for study and worship before the people. Administrative duties, important as they are, need to be shared with able laity who are searching for meaningful tasks other than the mundane ones often assigned to them.

Sixth, pastoral leadership needs to take more aggressive advantage of continuing education opportunities. The laity should insist upon it. The clergy's continuing education should be primarily in areas of weakness. No one needs to go to school to reinforce strengths; it's nice but not necessary. The pastor should seek the laity's help in appraising strengths and weaknesses. Religious leadership will enhance its credibility considerably through such consultations with the laity. Clergy engaged in continuing education through such a process are responding responsibly to their people, thereby increasing their accountability and deepening personal commitment and competence. In short, continuing education is the best insurance against theological malpractice among the people of God.

Seventh, religious leadership must cultivate spiritual life —the private interior dialogue with God. Clergy are known to pray for others, but praying in solitude is often neglected in a busy schedule. We all know that authentic piety is not the possession of any one class of persons; it needs to be cultivated and nurtured as do social concern and action. Prayer reminds us of who we are and the larger task before us. Discerning laity will listen to and be more willing to support the conscience and courage of religious leadership that is nurtured by a lively spirituality.

Loss of confidence can be restored. It will take time and listening on the part of all parties. The guidelines listed will help only to a limited extent. Expectations of the clergy and the clergy's expectation of the laity will need to be further resolved as the issues are faced realistically in a climate of mutual respect.

It is difficult to be realistic; this brings us to the task of relating theology to life, the concern of our next chapter.

2

The Tough Side of Ministry

Relating Theology to Life

In conversation with a newspaper editor, I suggested that loss of confidence in clergy leadership is a chief concern facing our churches today. The editor countered by saying that "loss of confidence is only an aspect of a deeper problem—namely, the problem of communication." He added that "religious leaders do not know how to package their concerns. They have made religion irrelevant to the marketplace." I protested, pointing to the religious ferment and searching in the marketplace. The editor nodded in agreement, but continued to insist that whatever authentic religious interest exists survives in spite of the clergy. The number-one problem faced by the church and its leadership, he felt, is to relate human concerns to religious values. "The clergy," said the editor, "need to rid themselves of meaningless 'buzz words' and begin to communicate where people are. Furthermore," he added, "the important thing is not what is said, but how it is said. It is the tone of the message that does the communicating." I left the conversation reflecting upon the "buzz words" of the clergy's vocabulary and the tone in which they are used. Perhaps the editor was overreacting; no doubt he was indicating why he himself was among the growing number who find the church irrelevant. But continued reflection upon the conversation indicated to me at least four lessons to be learned by pastors.

LESSON ONE: *Theology that does not wrestle with life issues is not worthy of people's attention in the marketplace.* Theology must be more than the sharing of ignorance. Theology must speak and give insight to the puzzling ambiguities and ethical choices confronted each day by individuals. The great temptation in seeking relevance is to tell people only what they want to hear. Relevance in practice so often is simply reinforcing the prejudices and biases found among parishioners. Relevance at this level quickly becomes irrelevant. The pastor becomes a defender or offender of the status quo, but in either case no more than a pawn among parishioners. Relating theology to life points to a deeper note of relevance—namely, relating biblical truth to the numerous gray zone areas in which we find ourselves. Applying the biblical truth will never be easy; trade-offs may even be necessary, but at least all parties involved should become aware of the pitfalls and rationalizing processes that dilute our commitments and convictions as believers. It is at this point that the pastor must be a clear and articulate voice who not only has something important to say at that moment but also through experience learns how to say it.

Many immediate issues need to be confronted: abortion versus overpopulation, environment versus jobs, gun control, morality, hunger, etc. Let us consider the issue of human survival as seen in the worldwide shortage of food. Does the pastor lead the congregation and influence the marketplace in this crisis? Providing Thanksgiving and Christmas baskets to the needy is not an adequate approach to this global and national problem. What kind of theological leadership can the pastor provide that will motivate a worthy response in the context of spreading scarcities and rising prices? Addressing this crisis is a problem that will face every pastor in our global village. The political leaders of our shrunken world are also now debating the ways and means of that survival. The fears of George Orwell's *1984* have paled into the background when confronted with the consequences of the year 2025. By 2025, there will be more people living than the earth can feed, given its present technology. This gloomy outlook has been forecast by numerous studies. It is clear we live in a hungry world in search of a new Garden of Eden. Does the local grass-roots theologian simply yield when faced with the magnitude of the problem?

To raise our consciousness as to the gravity of the situation, Gerry Connolly, of the American Freedom from Hunger Foundation, gives banquets that dramatize the current world food crisis. A feature story in *The Wall Street Journal* described the host waiting "for the ripe moment when stomachs are growling and heads ache from hunger before serving any food. Then one third of the guests sit down to juicy prime ribs, steaming baked potatoes and all the trimmings. The other guests are served a mound of rice and tea." Commenting on this tactic, Mr. Connolly notes that "the hostility of those two thirds eating rice and drinking tea is really something. For some people it ceases to be a game."[1] Survival never is a game when your own life is at stake.

Connolly's "hunger banquet" aims to arouse consciousness among the guests that there is a visceral bond between them and the undernourished two thirds of the world living with them in the global village. Also, the guests quickly grasp something of the anger of the hungry —especially toward the rich nations, which give away food when granaries are overflowing but are tightfisted in times of shrinking supplies. The anger is mostly directed toward the United States, as the 1975 World Food Congress in Rome revealed. We are viewed as the "Arabs of the world food supply." The outcome, predicts Georg Borgstrom, professor of food science and nutrition at Michigan State University, is that we are headed for a direct collision with the poor of the world.

Yet many of us are unable to see this interrelationship between our welfare and our neighbor's welfare. Our shortsightedness will invite violence, with devastating chaos for all of us. In a global village, made possible through science-based technology and mass communication, we must recognize the fact that fighting in any one sector of the village affects the rest of the human community. There is no escape from involvement in a global village. Arming with nuclear weapons and pursuing a policy of self-sufficiency will promote a global catastrophe more tragic than anything we have already experienced.

How, then, are we to survive as a global village? Many suggestions have been forthcoming. Gus Tyler, news columnist and labor leader, suggests that we have a core course on the Survival of the Species (SOS for short) in our colleges and universities. Such a course would indeed heighten awareness of our common peril. Unfortunately, most suggestions will fall on deaf ears; we are too preoccupied with our own private concerns and national ills. The corners of the global village, like the famine-stricken countries of Africa and the subcontinent of India, seem too distant and the task so large that we don't even know where to begin.

For the most part, we have dulled our guilt feelings through a series of rationalizations and token contributions channeled through our respective religious institutions and relief agencies. For most of us involvement stops there. Frankly, we are too wrapped up with personal agenda—seeking fame, power, or fortune—to do any more. We shouldn't be surprised or shocked when someday, out of desperation, the hungry majority tears down our estates, businesses, and orderly neighborhoods. On that day the riots and demonstrations of the 1960s will look insignificant in comparison.

Pope Paul VI, realizing what was happening in the world, called for a proportionate sacrifice of our resources and the possibility of placing these goods effectively at the disposal of the individuals and nations that need them, without any exclusion or discrimination. His threefold suggestion calls for a reorientation that would (1) increase production, (2) provide a more equitable distribution process, and (3) avoid waste and reduce the amounts of conspicuous consumption found among the world's affluent.

The wastefulness of our abundance was dramatized in a news story from Camarillo, California, where an elementary school principal in an agricultural community became distressed about pupils tossing most or part of their lunches into the garbage can. To dramatize the waste, principal Jerry Moynihan gathered the pupils and teachers of Pleasant Valley School around a picnic table during one lunch hour. He dumped the contents of the nearest trashcan onto the table. Sixth-grader Arlene Medina prepared the official inventory: "There were 41 sandwiches, two burritos, two cartons of milk, two whole pieces of chicken, three bags of potato chips, 19 apples, 13 oranges, one piece of cake, a half can of chocolate pudding, four carrot pieces, a piece of Mexican bread, two small boxes of raisins, 19 pieces of candy and 14 cookies."[2]

Highlighting our waste and conspicuous consumption may seem insignificant, given the size of our global problem. A Missouri cattle and hog farmer was quoted in a Meat Board publication as saying, "True, denying myself meat today does not put food in my Indian brother's bowl tomorrow, but with enough concerned people, enough trade and fair exchange programs, and generous national program of aid, it will make a difference in due time."[3] While the average American eats 14 pounds of fish, 51 pounds of poultry, 112 pounds of beef, 73 pounds of pork, and 300 eggs annually, most world citizens exist on much less. We could also live on less, feel better, and do more; overweight is one of the chief worries of affluent Americans.

Other means have also been suggested in meeting the food crisis: the creation of an international food reserve bank, increased efforts at family planning, the establishment of a new billion-dollar agriculture development fund, with monies contributed equally from oil and industrialized countries. All such programs are worthwhile and have merit in addressing a complex problem, which is further complicated by political and social factors in each section of the global village.

Yet all such efforts will not be enough, according to Garrett Hardin, professor of human ecology at the University of California. He insists that we must be more realistic and points out that "countries rich in grain would fill the granary and starving countries would empty it. This would amount to communizing food. Rich countries would have to work harder every year to meet the increasing demand of the rapidly multiplying poor countries. In the end, the rich countries would fall by the wayside as they too become poor."[4] His proposal is to oppose any formation of an international food reserve system and to tighten our immigration policies in the United States. "Unrestricted immigration," he says, "produces the same end result. By immigration, people are moved to the food rather than food to the people. The difference is relatively trivial."[5] Is he too harsh? Perhaps we have come to the end of our national tradition and the values inscribed on our Statute of Liberty: "Give me your tired, your poor, . . . the wretched refuse of your teeming shore . . ."

Professor Hardin's proposals, seen in a larger global perspective, will find sympathetic supporters among those favoring the triage theory, expounded by Dr. Philip Handler, president of the National Academy of Sciences. The word "triage" (French for "sorting out")—the system of sorting out the wounded in wartime: saving the savable, and neglecting the hopeless cases, as well as those who can recover without aid—has been revived in the current debate over the means for survival. In essence, the theory suggests that national leaders may have to agree that some of the world's hungry should be left to perish or fend for themselves in order that another portion may be fed and kept alive. The reported plan in India, for example, is to feed the cities, even at the expense of the rural areas. This is the triage theory in practice.

Dr. Handler estimates that 500,000,000 are presently on starvation diets in the world. Some 200,000,000 should be allowed to die so that 300,000,000 might be saved. This "lifeboat ethics" illustrates the impending tragedy of our day. Who would make the choices? Political considerations would be determining factors. Is this the most "realistic" approach to our problem? The debate over means becomes quite heated among the participants at this point. The responsibility for making decisions of such magnitude will eclipse previous genocides in human history.

What means should the churches choose in the debate over survival? Should churches begin to examine the limits and consequences of humanitarianism? Is generosity the best policy, or is it only a means of self-satisfaction? When is generosity a duty and when is it a contribution to increase distress in the future? What concepts of right and wrong should govern us? These and many other hard questions will need to be raised and resolved in the immediate future.

The answers to the above questions depend upon our basic assumptions toward life. The church, as an opinion-making institution in the larger society, must share its answers to these questions or further minimize its standing and contribution toward shaping public policy. From my perspective as a grass-roots theologian within the church, the following theological and biblical assumptions toward life should motivate the church's (and society's) strategies and actions:

1. Poverty will always be a part of the human drama. There are no shortcuts or ultimate solutions. However noble our goals, the biblical viewpoint informs us that during our earthly pilgrimage we will always be somewhat "east of Eden."

2. All are created in the image of God. Both rich and poor have like value in God's sight. God is no respecter of persons. The biblical outlook may not seem pragmatic, but a lesser commitment dehumanizes ourselves and defaces the image of God in each of us.

3. Creation itself is a loan from God. To misappropriate this loan leads to unfavorable consequences. We have been misusing our environment in behalf of short-term interests. A new village ethic demands that we take a second look, based upon the undeniable interdependence of God's creation. We live in a world without boundaries.

4. God expects us to practice justice, to love kindness, and to walk humbly with him. This biblical outlook commits us to pursue a policy of fairness; God's intention is that we minimize suffering and maximize self-fulfilling relationships in the global village. This is never easy. We are all in need of Solomon's wisdom. Once we are viscerally convinced of our global interrelatedness, however, we will begin to practice in larger measure a policy of fairness in behalf of global self-interest. Justice and kindness depend on a transformation of our existing structures.

Building upon the above assumptions, we can have a confident and realistic hope toward the future. In order for that hope to take concrete form we must encourage those efforts which meet the needs of the poorest of the poor in the Third World (what many are calling the Fourth World). We cannot simply dismiss, for instance, a Bangladesh as a hopeless international basket case. Jesus' commission to his disciples then and now remains the same: "As you do it to the least of these my brethren you have done it to me." This is why the living symbols of the Christian faith have been a cross, a shared meal, and a common prayer: "Our Father, . . . give us this day our daily bread." These symbols mandate our involvement in a hungry world.

As the global community draws together out of a sense of mutual self-interest, we will all discover that there can be no security for anyone in "lifeboat ethics," closed borders, or in illusionary isolated self-sufficiency. Survival depends upon an outlook that emphasizes the divine-humanity in everyone. The grass-roots theologian who can guide the people of God to work within the above guidelines has provided a framework for involvement. Such a framework is needed when our enthusiasm for doing good may wane or weaken for some short-term pragmatic consideration that may dehumanize us and deface the image of God in each of us. Theology that wrestles with essential life issues such as hunger will always find an audience in the marketplace.

LESSON TWO: *Theology must be a matter of not only verbalizing our faith but also the living out of our faith.* The Christian style of life is always a matter of word and deed. Sometimes we tend to forget this as we sit through committee meetings, boring each other with our "orthodoxy" and busyness. Ministry in its essence is the embodiment of that old and ever-contemporary story that God loves the world and is in the process of redeeming it. As grass-roots theologians we are an extension of that redeeming process, making our theological pronouncements incarnate in our locality. The doing of theology in concrete deeds will always be the most eloquent testimony of its relationship to life.

Sometime ago I asked a group of clergy in a summer school session to write a brief essay on the following question: "Can you picture Ralph Nader as your pastor?" The responses to the question were interesting and thought-provoking. The essay was an experiment on my part to see whether it was possible for us to grasp our mission better as pastors vis-à-vis a well-known crusader of consumerism like Ralph Nader. One pastor in the group replied in the following way:

> My first tendency was rather naturally to answer in the negative to this question because, as far as I know, Ralph Nader has no personal faith that is witnessed to publicly through his frequent pronouncements about "consumerism." And yet his seemingly selfless concern about the consumer in relationship to society may strike some resonant chords as well, in terms of a theological concern about man in relationship to his world.
>
> If one accepts the kind of thinking that even the practice of theology must begin at the point of meeting the needs and anxieties of man, then perhaps it could well be said that Ralph Nader could function in the context of a pastor, given that same kind of concern. In the respect that Nader is concerned as well about the basic stewardship of wealth and goods, it does not seem to me to be too far from there to a stewardship of life, which appears to be an essentially theological kind of orientation. Thus I can picture Ralph Nader as a pastor, with the assumption that his practice of law would become a practice of theology.

I can appreciate the above pastor's attempt to view Nader through the filter of one's own profession and discipline. I really don't know how much sense it would make to Nader. Be that as it may, the important thing that challenges us who are clergy is the ability of Nader to translate his concerns into deeds. He makes mistakes, he has enemies, but he also has the respect of countless millions who see him as an authentic doer of what he believes. No matter where we stand on Nader, his presence is a challenge to the grass-roots theologian to be a doer as well as a speaker of God's involvement in human life.

There are, of course, many doers among the clergy and among those committed to religious life. From time to time we pause and acknowledge the beauty of their lifestyle and witness. In our private thoughts we may view them as living saints. *Time* magazine noted the following examples of such living saints: Mother Teresa of Calcutta, Schwester Selma Mayer in Jerusalem, Archbishop Dom Helder Câmara in Brazil, Coptic monk Matta El Meskin in Egypt, Annie Skau in Hong Kong, and John Lewis in San Antonio.[6] There are, of course, many more unmentioned and unknown. These individuals are in the minority; the majority of us have tended to verbalize our faith, in the midst of our numerous priorities. Discipleship is costly; as with Jonah, the temptation is great to run from our own Nineveh rather than to answer the call of God to witness in *word and deed* unconditionally.

LESSON THREE: *Theology must translate its intimidating language and streamline its style into the idiom of the day.* It may surprise many a pastor to be told that theological jargon is intimidating to the congregation and the general public. Take, for instance, an often-used term like "theology." Have you ever asked a group of laypersons to define "theology" or at least to express how they understand the term? The responses will surprise you, but even more astounding will be the suspicions of some that you are trying to intimidate them with a "theological solution" to a contemporary issue. Every profession has its "in" language. I am not asking that we abandon all technical vocabulary. What we need to learn professionally, however, is a method of translating these technical terms into every-day vocabulary. We are all laity vis-à-vis one another's profession or trade; we need to remind ourselves of this constantly. Each professional's special vocabulary is intimidating to anyone standing outside that profession. The professional who is aware of this and consciously works to overcome this alienation is practicing the art of profession. Not only must the medical doctor practice the art of medicine along with the science of medicine, so must the pastor practice the art of ministry along with the science of ministry. The grass-roots theologian is regularly called upon to translate the language of theology. This involves a creative synthesis of the art and science of theology.

When such a synthesis is consciously practiced, the level of intimidation will be reduced, and ministry can take place. We will discover that there is also a need to streamline our theological doctrines to speak more meaningfully in the idiom of our day. Living in a technological world that knows no boundaries, the theological enterprise is desperately in need of unloading yesterday's inventory of formulas, divisions, and agenda in order to embark on new ventures. Such ventures call for a new style of theologizing, designed for more flexibility amid today's numerous revolutions—social, technical, and informational. To date, we have been traveling with cumbersome trunks laden with our theological past—a difficult position from which to meet the demands of a space age.

There will always be the inevitable struggle between continuity and discontinuity in facing the future. Obviously there are lessons to learn from the past, but our priority must be to theologize for the living rather than for the dead. We are a pilgrim people. Unfortunately, in the process we have forgotten that ours is also a pilgrim theology; our theologizing is never a finished product. We need to remind ourselves of its pilgrim status, lest we become too closely attached to our human foundations. Too often we have shown a settler's mentality—expending our energies and talents on maintaining territorial rights, which our traditions and confessions have led us to claim as being almost sacred. These churchly confessions are now under challenge by new consciousness fueled by our technical advances. Within this global, computerized, measured, and sophisticated environment, what shape will theology take in the future?

Tailored to our pilgrim status, our theologizing must be less encumbered in form. Our thoughts must capture the imagination of a technically oriented age, while the truth of our message must be faithful to our forefathers. We are living closer together today technologically, if not theologically. Nonparochial theologizing will be characterized by simplicity, avoiding excessive confessional baggage; we need somehow to travel lighter as pilgrim explorers. The communion of saints confessed in the Apostles' Creed already enjoys an unencumbered ecumenical fellowship that would be the envy of most of us. A unified awareness of humankind is now technically possible and necessary for our total survival; a theological oneness, however, remains remote as we safeguard our identities in our respective "hope chests," filled with yesterday's memories and suspicions. The theological task ahead for the future pastor is to create a *common hope chest,* to be helpful to those who have caught the urgency to "travel light" as pilgrim employers. In short, our theologizing must be succinct and expressive to hold and to extend our witness in tomorrow's global society.[7]

The marketplace is waiting for an increasing number of grass-roots theologians who can package their faith in simplicity without losing essence. Our confessions and theological books of the past have fulfilled a purpose and continue to be instructive. Like our forebears, however, we must have the pioneer's wisdom to travel without excess baggage if we are to free ourselves from the familiar shibboleths that are alien to the larger society. Our pilgrim outlook must also free us from excessive verbiage on our journey to liberate and be liberated. For too long now, we have been in a state of imbalance—overly weighted down with past traditions and unable to keep up with the living tradition personified in the Eternal Contemporary, Jesus Christ.

A pilgrim's theology, contained in a knapsack, indeed will free us to theologize as creative grass-roots theologians. Creative theologizing is always in tension between the pull of the past and the pressures of the present. Distorting this tension exclusively in any one direction will disguise reality and result in the heresy of reductionism. To place a period after our confessional and theological statements is to commit the error of reductionism. Global theologizing must responsively witness by daring to put no more than a semicolon behind our statements. Thus we will be both emotionally and intellectually better equipped to meet Christians and non-Christians in a world without boundaries.

LESSON FOUR: *Theology must seek to integrate the experiences and events of life into a meaningful framework under God.* To do so, the pastor must consciously work at being a theological integrator at the grass roots. Everyone is in search of a frame of reference in which to place the events and experiences happening throughout life. Since our theologizing will always be incomplete as a pilgrim people, the framework also will remain unfinished. In our search for meaning, we will never solve all the mysteries of life. Many tragedies in our lifetime will occur, and it will be difficult to find meaning in those tragedies. Our framework must be sufficiently flexible to include such tragedies. It is incumbent upon the grass-roots theologian to be a guide in helping persons to build a viable frame of reference under God. The pastor as theological integrator can perform a valuable service in freeing individuals from a sense of being locked in with their past. Exciting possibilities within the grace of God will open to those escaping a narrowly conceived framework. The pastor serving as theological integrator, in fact, will undergird and shape the congregation and the community at large to place again their trust in God in a meaningful way.

Individuals are searching for relational patterns of meaning between their thoughts and their daily experiences. Living in a highly fragmentalized and specialized society, the pastor as theological integrator can perform a socially unique role in building provisional bridges to stay in touch with our common humanity fashioned in the image of God. This need for integrators has been recognized among management and business personnel. There is active recruitment in industry for such individuals. Effective integrators in industry speak the language of each of the specialist groups, and thus are able to work at resolving interdepartmental conflicts.[8] The integrator with a cross-specialist perspective brings a dimension of insight that enables specialists to see beyond their ghetto. The pastor as integrator can serve a useful function by working for a level of unity among the compartmentalized elements within a community. Individuals need guidance to overcome their fragmented frames of reference. Each of us at times is blinded and deaf to the marvelous ways in which God's grace is operating in the lives of others. The pastor as integrator can provide an important overview position to help each of us in the community to transcend our tendency to bury ourselves within the ghetto of our "reality."

Discovering the Radical Nature of Faith[9]

One day Joe dropped by the office for a chat. Joe was a senior seminarian and a good student—the kind of person who contributes toward an instructor's own growth. I was glad he walked in.

"What's on your mind?" I asked. Joe looked rather pensive as he slumped into the easy chair and unfolded to me his increasing doubts about his Christian beliefs. The intensity and anxiety of his "confession" led to his searching cry, "I'm losing my faith!" Joe's concerns had been worrying him for some time. Joe, of course, is not alone. There are countless "Joes" in seminary, many reaching their senior year and harboring doubts that they refuse to reveal to fellow students and faculty.

The feeling of losing one's faith, while discussing the sacred materials of the faith, has always been a dangerous hazard in preparing for professional ministry. The phenomenon is not new; seminarians of yesteryear and those of today are confronted by the probing question, "What do I really believe?" The goal of seminary education is to answer that question. The responsibility of the faculty is not to undermine faith, but to help students to identify, articulate, and nurture a living faith.

Each year's entering class of seminarians has varied during my years of seminary teaching. One factor, however, remains the same: the large number of students who have made no distinction between faith and theology. The confusion in this area has caused some students to reach their senior year and then realize that they have refused an education. How to go through seminary without learning is almost the hidden wish of some students, who are actually afraid that the seminary process (a necessary means to obtain one's union card) will undermine their "faith." Not infrequently a seminarian will share with me the fact that a pastoral friend, a grandfather, or a saintly mother offered the parting advice, "Now, don't you let that seminary take away your faith!" The treasured relationship with a particular friend or relative who has implanted that type of advice often brings an implicit, if not explicit, suspicion toward the faculty and the seminary in general.

My own experience includes many seminarians with "clenched fists" defying the professor to take away their "faith." This attitude seeks to protect and keep alive the "faith" brought to the seminary. Without sufficient awareness of this factor, the instructor and the student can spend a whole semester bypassing each other through showers of verbiage. The instructor must depart from the agenda, and begin to construct a bridge of understanding by identifying and recognizing the "faith" that each student has and protects with a clenched fist.

This necessary process of identifying one's faith will facilitate fruitful dialogue where theologizing can flourish to the mutual enrichment of student and instructor. Often, as a student shares ideas and beliefs with fellow students in the classroom, a valuable informational and supportive climate results. It is incumbent upon the instructor to share also in this process. Slowly, one begins to see the clenched fists relax to open palms, signifying a spirit more receptive to learning.

Inevitably, the transition from fist to palm helps students to make an appreciative and also critical appraisal of the sources that have nurtured their faith to date. Without denying the vitality of previous experiences, or the trust placed by others, the student begins the slow but exciting process of identifying *the source* beyond the sources. This is theologizing and is at the heart of the theological enterprise.

The faith of each student who comes to seminary has been formulated and conditioned in numerous ways. For instance, the absence or presence of family devotions, grace at mealtimes, the testimony of a respected person or friend and the desire to emulate that person, a "decision for Christ" at an evangelistic gathering, a dogmatic statement or confessional creed, Sunday worship services, etc. One could go on to list many other sources, or what I would prefer to call "theological casings."

Seminary education is designed to take a careful look at all of these theological casings. The process of objectifying and identifying these casings can be rather painful for some students—it may appear at times as an outright attack upon an individual's "faith." This may not be true at all in the effort to separate faith from theology. "Faith" maintained in a clenched fist may well be protection for a theological casing that is outmoded and inadequate. A student like Joe may not notice "faith" slipping for lack of an adequate casing until late in the seminary career. Those students who have made the shift from fist to palm will, it is hoped, become aware of the fact that they are not losing their "faith," but shedding outmoded wrappings that are blocking the stream of living faith flowing from the past to the future. The casing process, unwrapping and wrapping, is the theologizing activity necessary for the communication of a vital faith.

Seminarians who feel that they are losing their "faith" often discover that they have been a parasite on someone else's struggle-filled pilgrimage. Consequently, some approach God in a second-hand manner. They come to God with borrowed crutches—theological casings that they have inherited or adopted. Should these borrowed crutches fail in a time of need, the feeling of losing one's "faith" becomes more pronounced. At times, this is accompanied by nostalgia for the comfortable past. Thus students threatened by the loss of their adopted crutches desperately seek some substitute crutch—something to satisfy their present needs.

In this pursuit from one set of crutches to the next, the pilgrim seminarian will begin to discover that living faith is communion with God without crutches. The call to come to God without crutches is so radical that students may refuse to accept the invitation, as they look frantically for some theological messiah to pull them through. Disappointment sets in when they discover how humanly limited all theological messiahs are. *There is really no escape from the radical nature of faith.* The truth is that God wants us to come to him without crutches of any kind. God alone is the *source* worthy of our full commitment. "I am who I am. There is none other."

Until the priority of this claim is firmly fixed in our guts as well as our heads, we will go on losing our "faith," as the inadequacy of all theological casings, past and present, is pointed out to us wherever rigorous theologizing is maintained. Seminary education is actually dedicated to helping us to lose our theologies without losing our living faith in the *source.* Philosopher Alfred North Whitehead perceptively stated that "religions commit suicide when they find their inspiration in their dogmas." This is true for Christianity, and Whitehead's definition of religion as "the denunciation of gods" can be appreciated. The seminary that is negligent in questioning the theological "gods" on the campus is shirking its positive responsibility to identify, articulate, and nurture faith in the living God.

At the same time, isn't this faith in the living God also a theology that must be questioned? Can there be a faith without a theology? Professor Schubert Ogden, of the Perkins School of Theology, has indicated that "faith without theology is not really faith at all, theology without faith is still theology, and quite possibly good theology at that."[10] In other words, the theological enterprise is a responsible intellectual exercise that need not presuppose faith. Faith in the living God is not necessary for theological discussion.

All faith statements, however, have theological implications based upon our spiritual experiences. Sharing these experiences always involves a tension between mystery and meaning. Too often it seems that seminaries tend to subordinate mystery in search of meaning. This may explain in part the decline of spirituality within our seminaries while, ironically, interest in spiritualism and the occult is increasing in society.

The Association of Theological Schools in its Task Force Report on Spiritual Development in theological education has recognized for some time this decline in spirituality and the resulting "crisis of faith" among seminarians.[11] This declining spiritual formation within our seminary communities is a widespread phenomenon in liberal, conservative, independent, and denominational seminaries. The fact that the decline is so widespread is to warn us against any simple solution.

The tension between mystery and meaning will exist as long as the seminary is both a professional academic center and a semimonastic center of meditation and prayer. This dual identity of the seminary fits the disposition of the modern seminarian. The future pastors are searching after a mystery in which they can believe. At the same time, they seek a functional place among human institutions through which they may expend intense energies with integrity and with renewing results for themselves and for the larger human community. The crucial question in the life of the seminary is whether one can prepare professional church leaders without destroying their authentic piety. Can the tension between the search for mystery and the search for meaning be maintained?

As a community, we must recover the radical nature of biblical faith that lies behind our distrust of structures, theological labels, and their limitations. In the light of The Letter to the Hebrews we must recapture our focus on faith as "the assurance of things hoped for, the conviction of things not seen" (Heb. 11:1, RSV). A faith in the living God must be reasserted within our theologies. Nicolas Berdyaev, the Russian philosopher, has rightly emphasized that theological doctrine is not necessary for faith, but that faith is necessary for theological doctrine. This implies that primacy should be given to spiritual experience over theological doctrine, for, in the last analysis, theology concerns spiritual experience.[12] Our spiritual experiences are not fully covered by explanations; our questions outnumber our answers. These are aspects of the unresolved tension between mystery and meaning. This is the nature of a pilgrim's theology.

Our wish to have answers for all our questions has tempted us to subvert our traditional theologies into crutches in our relationship to the living God. The truth is that God is beyond our grasp. The desire for an authoritative faith in our respective traditions has too often been a rationalizing attempt to "corner" God. "Let God be God" has been the reforming spirit of the church in every age. This spirit must be reaffirmed again and again to avoid entrapment in parochialism or the latest fad.

Our theologizing must always include an awareness of our limitations. Theologian Gordon Kaufman, of Harvard, has delineated the limits in all "God-talk."[13] When all is said and done, God is still *incognito,* beyond our grasp. Only through the biblical revelation do we in faith worship a God of grace and mercy. For the Christian, this God is most meaningfully understood in Jesus Christ. Yet God in himself is unknowable; he is beyond our means for verification. At most, we can have only an attitude of reverent agnosticism regarding his inner nature.

The Eastern Orthodox tradition has long taught that God in his essence is unknown; only his energies can be discerned. This has been reflected in their apophatic method of negative theologizing, as opposed to our more positive or kataphatic theologizing in the West.[14] The Easternization of Christianity, resulting from our increased global awareness, will encourage us to place limits on theological conclusions.

We must remember to let God be God and to let Jesus be Jesus, rather than harmonize the two beyond our human knowledge and implications. We must allow the

radicalness of faith, in the spirit of The Letter to the Hebrews, to permeate our witness as we communicate to
others the simplicity of faith. At seminary, we often lose
the art of being simple in our attempt to be academically
profound. We ignore the possibility that our theology may
be nothing more than educated ignorance at a higher
level of abstraction. The ministry in a sense is a profession
of learned ignorance based upon the testimonies of individuals in faith. Through private prayers, corporate worship, and the doxology we are reminded of the simplicity
of this faith, and also of the fact that our theological journey in life is never completed. Ours is a pilgrim theology
—of moving and of waiting—in response to the living
Lord.

All the evidence is not in, and no matter how earnestly
we try, the last word will be God's, not ours. This eschatological reality is our line of accountability. Living on this
side of that eschatological line of accountability should
humble us to limit our claims. We are reminded that all we
say and do is within the shadow of the divine Presence. It
is our task, then, to question all existing theologies, prone
as each is to the temptation of idolatry. By so doing, we will
maintain the radical nature of our faith. H. Richard Niebuhr, in his book *The Meaning of Revelation,* observed:
"Man as a practical living being never exists without a god
or gods; some things there are to which he must cling as
the sources and goals of his activity, the centers of
value."[15] Seminary education is designed to help us distin-
guish among the gods, that our faith may be solidly an-
chored in the living God.

In the course of my years of teaching, many students
have come to seminary and launched professional careers
in the ministry. The hope was that each would begin to
grasp the significance of separating faith from theology as
we sought together the living God behind our theologies.
The pastor must ever keep the importance of this separa-

tion in mind. Joe was not losing his faith, but rather deepening it—discarding theological casings he had brought to seminary. He had outgrown them, and the order of the day called for a new outfitting. In continuing his pilgrimage, he will be in need of further casings to embrace the enlarging breadth and depth of his faith in the living God. The pastor who operates within this framework will be of immense aid in helping others in their own search for the sacred. This is our vocation: to bear witness in the marketplace to the reality and presence of God in all dimensions of life.

Our next chapter focuses on the fact that an increasing number of Joe's future colleagues in ministry will be women.

3
Women and Men in Ministry

The Present Scene

The feminization of the clergy is a reality today. Only a few years ago I wrote about "the advent" of women pastors; that "novelty" is now an established fact. A recent study sponsored by the Ford Foundation declares unequivocally that "clergywomen have arrived."[1] The report indicates that 75 percent of women clergy have been in their parish ministry for six years or less, as compared to 15 percent of the men.[2] This trend of increased women clergy is certainly more than a fad; one third of the candidates in the United Presbyterian Church are currently women, and indications are that this will increase to one half by 1990. This example is repeated also in many other mainline denominations.

The reality of women clergy, however, continues to be met with mixed feelings, especially among the Anglican, Orthodox, and Catholic churches. These communions believe it is a violation of ecclesiastical and biblical tradition. Among Anglicans, for example, it has caused a good deal of tension. This has been evident on the American scene within the Episcopal Church (Anglican tradition) in the United States whose House of Bishops gently reprimanded four bishops who "irregularly" ordained eleven women as priests. The church declared the women's ordination invalid. The issue was reconsidered at the Minneapolis General Convention of the church, which voted by a slim margin in favor of the full ordination of women to the priesthood, a practice not yet officially accepted by the Anglican Church in Great Britain.

There has been also a good deal of agitation among sisters in religious orders of the Roman Catholic Church. A well-publicized conference was held in Detroit on the theme "Women in the Future Priesthood Now: A Call for Action." Sister Marie Augusta Neal told the gathering that women will become priests when they begin to make decisions at every level of church structure. Sister Neal said that decisions currently are made in the church with "the limited vision of an all-male perspective on the world." She indicated that women must seek to enter into the decision-making process to widen church perspective and to mold a new type of priesthood that is open to women.[3] The official church has set up all-male game rules, which must change if the present "clerical culture" is to welcome women.[4]

In spite of the fact that one third of the constituent churches of the World Council of Churches now ordain women, the "all-male game rules" continue to prevail. The Orthodox churches, for instance, look askance upon the number of Protestant churches in the Council which are ordaining women. Georges Barrois, professor of Old Testament at St. Vladimir's Orthodox Theological Seminary, sums up the Orthodox sentiments against the ordination of women based upon their studies of Scripture and church history. According to him: "A mere survey of biblical evidence is not sufficient for solving the problem conclusively, for the Scriptures are not to be read independently of Tradition, the *paradosis*, which is the organ of divine revelation, and lives in the traditions of the Church. Tradition is necessarily influenced by historical and cultural contingencies; if it were not so, our teaching would be gratuitous ideology resting on shaky foundations."[5]

Barrois goes on to observe that cultures do have a life of their own. "History records their birth, their growing to maturity, their eventual obsolescence, and their extinction. Yet they are an integral part in the very texture of Church tradition and must not be forgotten or brushed aside. The life of the Church may call for new forms, but these shall have no chance if they are not traditionally rooted. This is why, if I am asked bluntly whether, in my opinion, women should be ordained to the priesthood, I will, even if I seem to overstep the limits of this essay, give an equally blunt answer: no!"[6] There is no ambiguity in Barrois' stance; his conclusion, if not his reasoning, gives comfort to the leadership of those church traditions opposed to women's ordination.

According to a *Los Angeles Times* report, the Vatican has quietly initiated a study on the ordination of women, even though officially the traditional doctrine of the Roman Catholic Church, like that of the Orthodox, is opposed to such ordination.[7] Many informed Catholic observers believe that Catholics will ordain women before the issue of celibacy in the priesthood becomes optional in the life of the church. In Reform Judaism there are now women rabbis. Shelby Rooks, president of Chicago Theological Seminary, has forecast that with more women and minorities attending theological schools, the white male is slowly disappearing from the future clergy job market.[8] In short, women clergy are definitely present, or are being considered, across all traditional and ecclesiastical boundaries today.

Basis for Women's Ordination

No matter how well established our sources of authority, the interpretative task will always confront the church's theologians. We cannot escape the responsibilities of interpretation; and all explanations will be less than definitive. How one interprets the Bible—not only what the text meant when it was written, but also what it means "here and now"—will always be a matter of tension for us. Hermeneutically, the biblical view that weighs the heaviest for me is the principle that *in Christ there is neither male nor female.* There is oneness and wholeness in Christ. The reconciling process points us to an organic whole in which male and female are one. Christ as the Second Adam has reunited us, as God in creation intended. Our mission in life is to be part of this reconciling process which Jesus pioneered for us with the unqualified giving of his life. Biblical passages that suggest the subordination of women are not the essence of the biblical revelation, if ultimate intent is reconciliation and oneness in Christ. This, then, is my vantage point for believing on biblical grounds that God wills the equality of males and females.

As contemporary disciples we must not be so "locked in" by our traditions that we are "locked out" of the continuing tradition found in the living Lord of the church, who wills reconciling oneness for us. The church as a living organism will always find itself in tension between its desire to seek reconciliation and the continued practices that divide us. Our living tradition in Christ is constantly being unfolded and expanded by the Holy Spirit, the Comforter and Challenger, who enables us to look beyond our present structures. It is from this Spirit-inspired content of openness and trust that the churches have been able to add and to subtract from their respective traditions. Any evidence, pro or con, on the issue of women's ordination based on whatever grounds (biblical, theological, ecclesiastical, sociological, psychological, or historical) must be weighed against an honest appraisal of our true intentions and aspirations. The ruling establishment within each ecclesial tradition (which today is male oriented) must be on guard against the subtle practice of hypocrisy shrouded in the name of tradition. In retrospect we know there is a real temptation to be flexible in interpretation in order to slant conclusions to our prior bias.

It is my own conviction that women should be ordained; there are strong biblical and theological grounds.[9] Furthermore, experience indicates that women clergy are beneficial for the church in its witness to the world. Men and women in pastoral partnership present a united front in a fragmented society that is suffering from broken relationships. Healing and reconciliation among men and women within the body of Christ illustrate that the church understands something about suffering and brokenness. As we work through our suffering experiences, we will promote both communion and communication among ourselves which in turn can lead us toward authentic community. Women have been at the center of much human suffering and as a result have additional understanding, as catalysts of the Spirit and as pastors, to help us overcome the strained relationships in our world today.

No doubt the male pastor will sometimes feel threatened by his female counterpart, especially if opportunities are limited. The female pastor for the immediate future will be frustrated as she discovers time after time that the church at the grass roots is not always an equal opportunity employer. But as both sexes work through this period of transition, the church twenty-five years from now will have leadership that more closely reflects the constituencies of the churches and their concerns. There also may be a rise in the number of clergy couples in the future as there are in other professional fields.[10] Congregations with a pastoral combination of male and female will be especially rewarded in a rich and full ministry.

Partnership in the church's future leadership must consist of males and females. Baptism brings men and women into God's family with equal status. We must further this inclusive and joyful community of mutual respect, equality, and partnership. Today's church has a predominance of women under male leadership; tomorrow's church, with a larger percentage of female leadership, will, I hope, redress the imbalance and motivate a larger percentage of male participation. Women pastors will raise the sensitivities of fellow clergy and the laity to neglected or misunderstood areas of need found in the marketplace. Some basic areas may include ministry to families and to youth. Men and women pastors must specialize in these areas and encourage parishioners to minister also.

The Future Family: Emerging Ministries

Twenty-five years from now the nuclear family will still be with us. Is the pastor aware of the implications of this fact? The nuclear family with a wife, husband, and one or more children will continue to be the basic model of tomorrow's family. It will be a smaller family in size, because of more sophisticated birth control measures, wider acceptance of abortion, and concern for more personal self-fulfillment. These projections are primarily aimed at middle-class life, although somewhat different patterns may also exist. The number of nuclear families among the married middle-class population will be somewhat reduced from today's level because of the following factors:

1. Childless couples will increase in number.
2. The percentage of single-parent families will increase.
3. Reconstituted families, where one or both spouses are in a second marriage, will increase. There will be more divorces in the future, influenced in part by the wider practice of no-fault divorces. Presently, there are 48 divorces for every 100 marriages. By 1990, based on present trends, there will be 63 divorces for

every 100 marriages. Many of these divorces will lead to second and perhaps more stable marriages.

4. The number of three-generation families, extended kinship families, may increase for financial reasons.

5. Experimental patterns of family life, such as sexually open marriages, heterosexual cohabitation, gay unions, intimate networks of communes and group marriages, will increase and be more visible to the public. The percentage rise will not be as great as its exposure and publicity through the media would indicate.[11]

Notwithstanding these above-mentioned factors, I strongly suspect that the nuclear family will continue to serve as the essential model of tomorrow's family. It will stand as the main trunk of the family tree; the factors mentioned above may be various branches or twigs of that tree.

The nuclear family can expect to change its life-style appreciably in the future. One of the major factors causing change in the family structure is the convergence of the women's movement and the rising cost of living. Women want their equality, and rightly so. At the same time, the cost of running a household is more than a single breadwinner can manage. The convergence of these factors has led to the dramatic rise in the number of adult women at work—more than ever before. From 1947 to 1975, the number of working wives increased 205 percent (from 6,502,000 to 19,835,000). In 1947, working husbands outnumbered working wives by nearly five to one. By 1975, this ratio was less than two to one.

It is important to note that among wives who work, the highest percentage is that of wives who have school-age children. The prime reason for their working is to help support the family, although their personal feelings for identity and liberation are also factors. The actual percentage of working wives with school children rose from 26

percent in 1948 to 51.2 percent in 1974. We have signifi-
cantly passed the midpoint, with more than half the wives
with school-age children either holding jobs outside the
home or looking for such jobs. With every indication that
this trend has continued, new pressures are felt by the
"liberated household" confronted with economic realities
and materialistic goals. The nuclear family will need to
rethink its values and priorities in the years ahead if it is
to maintain its sanity as the societal merry-go-round tends
to move faster and faster, consuming more of everything.

As the nuclear family reassesses its life-style in a con-
sumer society, it will ask, how much affluency is healthy for
family life? What are the necessities of life, and how are
these measured? How have today's necessities shifted from
our grandparents' day? Are today's needs considered luxu-
ries by yesterday's standards? Because of our present rate
of consumption, we have become dependent upon two
paychecks in the family; both spouses need to provide
income to increase the household cash flow. The marriage
vow of the bride, as well as the groom, may need to be
altered in the future to "love, honor, and financially support" the spouse. Big-ticket items such as automobiles and
homes are causing a larger number of families to discover
that it is no longer possible to live on a single paycheck.
Women's liberation has come none too soon. The feminist
movement provides for male liberation as well. Men can
relax somewhat now that the financial load is not entirely
theirs alone. Wives as allies can help to put bread on the
table.

Does this new parental liberation also spell liberation for
the children? The liberated household with a working
mother and father could lead to a victimized childhood for
someone abandoned to a day-care center, a neighbor, or
a relative. The introduction of a "third parent," on the
other hand, may bring a measure of liberation and hope
to a child whose parents are not equal to or desirous of the

task of child rearing. Dr. Robert S. Morrison, a Cornell University biologist, has pointed out that equal opportunity for persons must start at the crib. He says, "It is idle to talk of a society of equal opportunity as long as that society abandons its new comers solely to their families for their most impressionable years." Is it true that one of the unchallenged injustices in our day is the fact that one cannot choose one's parents? A creative and responsible day-care center or some other suitable alternative may well improve a child's chances for a more meaningful future. A partial loosening of the intensive emotional demands within the middle-class nuclear family may help create less-dependent personalities. It is, however, difficult to make general statements in this area; each case must be determined on its own merits. Giving birth is no longer a duty; it is a privilege with joys and limitations.

Increased outside influence upon the child and absent parents who are working will tend to promote a home atmosphere that is decentralized. The family in the year 2000 will express a greater spirit of equality between husbands and wives, parents and children.

With many families having both parents in jobs outside the home, with greater influence and assistance from child-rearing agencies, and with a more egalitarian atmosphere at home, what shape will family life take in the years ahead? There is the feeling among some observers and forecasters that these projected trends will lessen the commitment that family members will have to each other. There is the thought that the nuclear family as we have known it will be seriously threatened. I disagree. One reason is that people will be getting married later in life, providing the base for more stable marriages and a clearer sense of personal identities. Even more important, society's basic commitment to monogamous relationships will still be intact in the year 2000. We are a more conservative society than the headlines of our newspapers are willing to admit. As long as most families continue to meet the basic needs of individuals—food, shelter, love, loyalty, and a basic acceptance of persons in spite of their behavior—the nuclear family does have a future.

We will need, however, to expand our definition of the nuclear family to include single-parent families and extended kinship families as well. The nuclear family must avoid communicating a sense of suburban elitism among family groupings. Special attention must also be given to combat racism that especially focuses on children of mixed races. An expanded concept of the nuclear family as an institution where mutual love and forgiving take place on a day-to-day basis is essential in humanizing life around us.

The family in the year 2000 will accept more help from outside agencies. It will understand that assistance in child rearing will have positive benefits for the child that will outweigh the disadvantages. The discriminating family will be careful to regard any outside agency as no more than a source of assistance. The primary caring-loving role and the basic economic support will belong to the family.

The family of the future will be engaged more systematically in assessing its values and priorities. To operate as a liberated household, the family will never cease struggling with the question of human rights within the household. Each member's concern must be heard. Failure to listen will endanger the inner fabric of the family. The family will not have attained happiness in the year 2000 but will still be pursuing it as did its forebears. One hopes the nuclear family will come to realize that happiness is much more than satisfying the material needs of the household, necessary as they are. The family's pursuit of happiness will continue to be that magnetic force which will solidify and propel the family through times of difficulty and success. Tomorrow's family will need its dreams and visions as we do today. In any assessment of its goals, the family will feel greater pressure to discipline and simplify its life-style.

Affluence and waste must be curbed. A more modest and wholesome standard of living will be maintained for environmental as well as economic reasons.

The nuclear family in 2000, as a result, will be looking for greater cultural enrichment from colleges, universities, and community organizations. Why can't colleges and universities design programs and courses in continuing education for the *whole* family to attend? With late marriages and earlier retirements in the years ahead, there will be time and opportunity for parents, grandparents, and children all to be enrolled in courses together. Such common activity will enhance the quality of family life tomorrow. The U.S. Department of Labor indicates that retirement in the future will be mandatory by the age of forty. At the same time, life expectancies have risen from age forty-seven in 1900 to age one hundred by the year 2000. With these additional new blocks of time available, colleges, universities, churches, and community organizations should plan projects and programs to expand and enrich the entire community.

To summarize, the family in the year 2000 will not be dead. The nuclear family is certainly changing, but its demise is hardly likely, given the continuing philosophical, legal, and theological assumptions of our society. We are far more conservative than we are willing to admit. We have a greater propensity for continuity than discontinuity. Our present affluence will be carefully evaluated; families that merely provide dormitories and quick-food service will be criticized. Our merry-go-round pace of living will be deliberately slowed as increased periods of time become a new resource in the future. Along with more day-care centers, the government will seek to provide some kind of guaranteed family income to sustain a basic standard of human dignity through the family.

Yes, the family will be with us twenty-five years from now—less romanticized, perhaps, having tossed aside definitions of "the perfect family." Members of the household will be more accepting and less demanding of one another. The family will be less elitist and suburban in disposition as the concept of the nuclear family expands and becomes more inclusive of additional life-styles also seeking to establish family life. Finally, the family in 2000 will be more open to having personal needs for intimacy and commitment met in a greater variety of ways, outside the family as well as within the family. It will be more conscious than ever of our global nearness and interdependence upon each other in God's shrinking universe.

Among community organizations, I would like to think that the family in the year 2000 will make better use of the church than it does today. The future pastor who is awake and imaginative to the trends ahead will create a climate where goals and values of life can be more easily and openly discussed. The church, sensitive to the shocks and confusion ahead, can provide the family with a larger community, an extended family of relationships, that will stimulate and support the home.

In the church's strategy for tomorrow, it will be necessary for more clergy to receive specialized training in preparing themselves to be bona fide family counselors. Since every church will not be able to provide a pastor who is also a family counselor, it well might be to the community's interest to support financially such a trained pastor on an ecumenical basis. The churches will also need to develop a greater number of pastors as youth specialists who can also be ecumenically employed. Churches will be better able to fulfill the needs of tomorrow's families if there is greater economic and ecumenical cooperation to develop these specialized ministries. Without this kind of specialization, the churches will not be able to serve successfully as extended families in aiding tomorrow's family in its assessment of values and goals.

These specialized ministries to the family and to youth

will be wonderful opportunities of service in a market-place calling for help. This will be especially true in rural and small-town areas. Usually one can find specialization in the urban and suburban communities, but not in small-town and rural communities, which at times tend to be overchurched, while the real needs of the people are unattended. The pastor who has a certified speciality in family counseling or adolescent psychology can bring along with theological awareness a synthesis and approach that churchgoers in the community can trust and respect. It is my own feeling that men and women pastors, especially the latter, who prepare themselves to serve in this way can bring a liberating dimension of ministry to a community caught within a male caste system and suffering from boredom and impatience. A woman pastor who specializes at this point can minister to needs neglected and/or unnoticed by male clergy. She can also heighten the sensitivities of her fellow clergy to these needs. If we begin now to invest ourselves heavily in these areas of emerging ministries, future families will find the church to be an integral part of their life-style.

New Freedom for the Pastor's Spouse

Having women as grass-roots theologians points also to a greater liberation for the pastor's spouse. Since the spouse can be either husband or wife, we will need in the future to speak more broadly than the "pastor's wife." Of course, statistics indicate that pastors' spouses are still primarily wives. Therefore, I will direct my present discussion to the wives of pastors, and expect husbands of pastors to extrapolate (as so often has been the task of women).

Many a pastor's wife has remained cheerful while willingly (or grudgingly) being victimized as an unpaid servant of the church. Often feeling oppressed, she has been cautious and cooperative while lonely and frustrated. The right of women and the rising number of women pastors have brought the pastor's wife to a new threshold of self-awareness; she no longer harbors guilt for her needs of personal identity.

To be the wife of a professional is both satisfying and frustrating. There is both status and loneliness in such a situation. It would be instructive and therapeutic for the wives of professionals in several fields to meet and discuss together their woes and pleasures. Many will be sharing the same conflicts and problems. So often the wife of a pastor feels particularly exploited. Seen from a broader perspective, however, her joys and problems are shared by a wider circle of wives married to professionals. For example, Dr. James L. Evans, of the Institute of Living, in Hartford, Connecticut, has indicated that wives of medical doctors are often deeply troubled. According to him, doctors' wives are suddenly faced with a new set of problems as they become thirty years old, after the struggle associated with medical education and training and launching a career has ended. These women have been attracted to men with a profession but are later disturbed by such reality factors as the increasing involvement of their husbands in work and the conflict between their husbands' personality characteristics and the wives' idealized expectations.

The same phenomena can be observed among the wives of business executives. *The Wall Street Journal,* in several lead stories, underlines the fact that wives of executives pay a heavy price for their husbands' success.[12] Take, for instance, the case of the executive living in a comfortable home with three children, two cars, but a bitterly unhappy marriage. As their income grew, his hours away from home increased. The wife is suffering from deep-rooted sexual dissatisfaction, and her husband is the victim of sheer exhaustion from long hours and worry about his job. According to Allied Van Lines, which moves many executives around, the number of families in similar situations is considerable. Corporation executives have been known to move as many times as a pastor's family; both are conditioned to a nomadic existence. The women's movement has encouraged more of these frustrated wives to pursue careers and seek satisfying jobs as part of the answer in the midst of dissatisfaction and loneliness. Yet working partners with two careers can also be a new source of frustration if the fundamental understandings and goals of each party are not based upon a common consensus. Liberation involves more than material security or pursuing a career. Both are certainly factors in one's well-being, but a wife's liberation (as well as her husband's) can come only when each discovers the quality of relationship they wish to have with each other.

The primary relationship of a wife to her husband and a husband to his wife needs to be under constant review. Nothing should be taken for granted. The tendency of most partners married to professionals is to blame the profession for the dissatisfactions that might later result in the breakup of the marriage relationship. This is true for the wives of many clergymen who often feel victimized by their husbands' profession. In London, the wife of an Anglican clergyman is reported to have said that "clergymen should be celibates because being married to one is a lousy job." According to her, she had married seven years earlier with the high-minded vision of working with her husband in a great venture. "But here I am, surrounded by four children, tied to the house, expected to turn up at every cat-hanging, and feeling like a widow as my husband is always on duty." She goes on to say: "I resent also the double standards maintained in the parish. A clergyman's wife is expected to run the conventional things, turn up at church and every other connected social affair, whatever her domestic circumstances may be. One receives no encouragement for managing it, but plenty of blame when one does not. I also resent the fact that I have to be myself, self-consciously. If I 'twist' at the parish dance, this causes comment. I now have become so introspective that I ask myself if I 'twist' in order to cause comment. I resent the basic reason behind it—that somehow we are different. Clergymen ought to be celibate because no decent, right-minded man ought to have the effrontery to ask any woman to take on a lousy job. It is thoroughly unchristian." I wonder how many wives of clergymen would to some degree echo her sentiments. She certainly does not seem free or liberated.

Another case is found in a letter sent to Ann Landers from an unhappy pastor's wife.

Dear Ann Landers:
I have written you dozens of letters and torn them all up, but I promised myself that this letter is going into the mailbox.

I am a pastor's wife who is sick of the demands made on me and my family. There are approximately 500 members in my husband's congregation and approximately 500 ideas on how a pastor's family should live.

My husband puts in at least 70 hours a week, yet there is never a free evening just for us. We must visit the sick, visit the bereaved, visit the couple who had a new baby, visit the old woman who fell down and broke her hip.

The phone rings in the middle of the night. Mrs. So-and-So's husband is an alcoholic and he hasn't been seen since 3:30 P.M. A widow is worried about her teen-age son. He took the car without permission and she is sure he is dead in a ditch. A hysterical neighbor phones to say her daughter has locked herself in the bathroom and is threatening suicide.

Yesterday my husband received a letter criticizing the dress I wore Sunday. It was too short. Also, I had on too much lipstick. I am expected to serve on all sorts of committees. It is assumed that I will pour tea and stand in the receiving line of every civic and social affair.

Some nights I think my feet will fall off.

When I married my husband, I wanted to help him serve God, but in the 18 years he has been in the ministry I haven't seen even one life changed because of our efforts.

I hope you won't think I'm mercenary, Ann, but I bitterly resent the fact that we will never own our own home and we will always have to scrimp to make ends meet. The cost of living has skyrocketed in the past 10 years, but my husband's salary is the same as it was in 1958. He is a brilliant man, and we know we could have lived much better if he had chosen any other profession.

Please give a word of encouragement.

—Losing Heart[13]

Ann Landers was not able to help "Losing Heart." The famed columnist hoped some other pastor's wife who had worked through a similar situation would respond. A few months later, Ann Landers printed a response to "Losing Heart" from another pastor's wife of twenty years' experience.

Dear Losing Heart:

When I married I was determined to be the most universally loved minister's wife in the world. I soon learned it was impossible.

I tried playing the role of Fashion Queen. The criticism was scathing. I then tried dressing more conservatively, and was carped at for looking "down at the heels." When I ran myself ragged with committee work I was accused of trying to be "the center of everything," so I cut back on community work and did very little. I was then hauled up short for my indifference—even called "snooty."

My first three years as a pastor's wife were nightmarish. I felt as if I had failed miserably and was on the verge of a nervous breakdown. It took a lot of nerve but I decided to talk over my problems with another pastor's wife, one who was handling her life beautifully. She set me straight. Her advice was: "Stop trying to play a role. Be yourself. The person who tries to please everyone pleases no one."

Now I dress to please myself and my husband. I am deaf to remarks that my skirt is too short, my lipstick is too bright, or my hair is piled too high.

I never pour at teas or serve on committees unless I truly want to. If a cause doesn't appeal to me I don't become involved. I'm so busy with activities that do inspire me that I no longer feel guilty if I don't give a piece of myself to everything.

My husband is still overworked, but I've learned how to make our time together count. You can be sure I'm not the most popular pastor's wife in the world, but I now have a genuine sense of joy and fulfillment. I would not change places with any woman I know.

—Columbus, O.[14]

What had the experienced pastor's wife, "Columbus, O.," learned? What enabled "Columbus, O. " to be herself? An underlying assumption in a working marriage partnership should be the mutual desire on the part of each partner to help the other to be herself or himself. This goal should prevail in the relationship (and for that matter within the family) in order to create an atmosphere in which each seeks to fulfill and complement the spouse. The liberation movement, sexually, politically, and socially, aims to help persons individually and collectively to realize their identity, their personhood. It also acknowledges that we cannot do this without the help of one another.

Sexual distinctions between male and female symbolize the interdependence that exists between the sexes. A similar interdependence exists theologically between us and God. An individual's awareness of independence is in direct ratio to his or her awareness of dependence. This is another way of saying that none of us is perfectly free.

Freedom must be seen within the context of relationships. The old warning to a groom during the wedding rehearsal that he is about to lose his freedom simply isn't the case. In a healthy marriage, partners don't lose their freedom but actually extend freedom.

Most human beings at birth symbolically are given a "dog tag" by the hospital attendants. This dog tag identifies the infant and links the baby to the parents. For some years the parents hold the leash. In marriage the individual makes the choice with another person, causing the parents to release their leashes, thus enabling the couple to tie their separate leashes together. This gives the couple a wider span, a larger radius of coverage than the single leash either of them possessed prior to marriage. In a mutually growing relationship, one actually extends and widens movements and freedom rather than curtailing them. However, none of us is free of "dog tags" or "leashes." Our freedom always has strings (or some kind of relationship) attached to it. We have some choice as to the relationship (the strings), but no viable choice to think of ourselves as nonrelational entities. We all live with relational limitations, though admittedly our capacity and potential within any relationship are never fully realized.

Our freedom (our radius), then, is the measure of movement from our base. Is our base (our relational ties) providing us maximum movement or are we getting tied up into knots and shortening our potential distance of movement? In a healthy marriage, tying oneself with another person, becoming an extended radius, will, it is hoped, enable each partner of that relationship to know greater freedom and thereby to be enriched.

Marriage represents, perhaps better than any other expression of communal living, the fact that no individual is an island. To be a person is to understand oneself as a communal being, with an essential will to community. There is this constant need for fulfillment and completeness which every couple should seek to work out together. The goal of the couple is the mutual fulfillment of each other. In practice, this will result in trade-offs and compromises within a context of love. Witnessing maximum completeness of one's mate will bring fulfillment and satisfaction to each partner. Successful marriages are experiments seeking a creative balance at precisely this point. Where the balance is not always maintained, as in the case of many busy professionals, disturbances and doubts set in. The problem basically lies with the couple in renewing their efforts at communication, either directly together or, when necessary, with the help of a counselor. Only in a secondary way does the problem lie with one's profession or career. In the long run, the couple must find their balance, the fulfilling or complementing of each other in a satisfying way, if their marriage is to be a rewarding experience.

From this perspective, how should we look at the role of a minister's wife? Is there something "extra" asked of her? It is my contention that insofar as she conceives of her role as a minister's wife as being something "extra" or more than her primary relationship of fulfilling or complementing her life's partner, she is likely to face disappointment and unhappiness. She will be under constant anxiety and tension, giving her attention to secondary tasks, which divert her from being herself in those relationships where she chooses to spend her time and energies. It is at this point that the couple must have honest communication with each other, if maximum freedom and fulfillment are to be realized by each of them. This whole process becomes even more complicated when the entire family is taken into consideration. Reassessment of every situation and each relationship must go on regularly.

When the couple and their children understand each other, then the forces of society and the congregation will not persuade them to dance to half a dozen tunes of public opinion, never satisfying any of them. To reach this understanding, the pastor's wife may find herself to be the necessary catalyst who takes the initiative and expresses her freedom in order to get the process of open conversation started at home. As she creatively works out her own lines of interdependence, she will experience a measure of freedom without guilt, no longer seeing herself as the proverbial victimized wife of a pastor and his congregation. Her initiative will also enable her husband to work out his lines of interdependence, thus liberating him as well, no longer tempted to prostitute his wife for the church's program.

Within this context, it becomes clear that most of our conversation regarding a pastor's wife is carried on at a superficial level. Most discussions and materials written on the minister's wife attempt to ascertain in some quantitive way her relationship to the congregation. Such an approach often sees the minister's wife as a de facto "assistant pastor" to the congregation or as the "professional lay worker" in the life of the church and community. However, the question is not really a matter of degree at all, but rather a qualitative matter of relationship; how much or how little she should be involved in the church's life is not significant. She has a choice in her primary relationships. Any additional involvement outside the circle of her primary relationships is hers to determine in partnership with her spouse.

Of course, the primary circle of relationships can become an ingrown affair. To avoid this, the couple must continually see themselves (as should all the couples of the congregation) not only in interdependence upon each other, but constantly acknowledging the source of their mutual dependence upon the God who upholds us all. The committed couple will submit their activities and decisions to the wisdom of God, thus enabling them to be mindful of their own parochialness and self-centeredness. This transcended perspective will further free them to listen to others in love, not out of duty but from a liberated spirit of personal identity and self-fulfillment.

In the next chapter, we will need to place the pastor's spouse within the larger body of the laity and view the role of the laity alongside the pastor.

4

The Leadership of the Laity

Can the clergy expect greatness from the laity? Perhaps discussion on church leadership should have begun with this question. It may have been my failing with that business layman not to have asked him whether the clergy could expect greatness from the laity. Many times I have heard it said among my colleagues that their goal in ministry is to work themselves out of a job. There are at least two hidden assumptions behind that statement. First, that there can't be a church without an active laity. Second, that there can be a church without clerical leadership. I agree with the first, but take exception to the second. In actuality, *there can no more be a church without laity than there can be a church without clergy.* Laity and clergy are both essential to the church's well-being and mission. The laity are searching for compassionate and competent clerical leadership. By the same token, clergy are searching for committed and talented laity. We can never ignore this basic duality of church leadership. This duality of leadership with its resulting joys and tensions will continue in the future. The greatness expected of clergy is equally expected of laity. The saints and martyrs who typify the greatness of the church's early leadership were largely among the laity.

A Short History

Since the early part of the fourth century, the Christian church has been living in a post-Constantine era. Prior to Emperor Constantine's reign, the primitive Christian church was viewed largely as a *lay movement*. The church was predominantly a minority movement among the people of that day and was looked upon with disapproval by official Judaism as well as by imperial Rome. Followers and disciples among the Christians were seldom from the so-called priestly class of that day. Unlike John the Baptist, Jesus was not born of a priestly family. When the time came to trace his ancestry, the Evangelist stressed a royal rather than a priestly lineage. Yet, seeing in Christ the eternal High Priest (Heb. 4:14), early Christians came to think of themselves by virtue of their baptismal incorporation into him—priest, prophet, and king—as constituting collectively a priestly kingdom (Rev. 1:6) and a royal priesthood (I Peter 2:9), and as such carrying into the world the promises and the prerogatives of the ancient people *(laos)* of God (I Peter 2:10).[1]

Clement of Rome was the first Christian writer to use the term "layman," approaching the popular use of our day. Prior to Clement, in Acts 1:15 and 6:5, we see the apostolic church practicing a unified concept of the people of God, seeing the whole body as being directly involved in witness, in service, and in the election of their clerics or leaders. Also, the popular ascription of the power to forgive sins long remained associated with lay confessors, still evident in the lay monks within the life of the Eastern church. We note, also, that such outstanding teachers in the ante-Nicene period as Justin Martyr and Origen were laymen unordained as to priestly ministry. However, following the reign of Constantine, the role of the laity, the people of God, as such, decreased. The church became increasingly clergy dominated, especially in the West. The clergy syndrome of dominance has largely characterized the post-Constantine era to the present day.

Cyprian's famous dictum in the post-Nicene period was evidence of this when he wrote, "The Church is where the Bishop is." The elevation of the ordained priesthood had begun, and reached its peak during the Middle Ages. With the exception of a few aggressive emperors, the affairs of the church were largely controlled by the "professional worshiper"—the clergy. With the opportunities of education limited for the most part to clergy and the wealthy, plus the added factor of centralized sacramental worship in the church, the term "laity" referred to nonclergy who in fact experienced a second-class status as Christians. The biblical concept of *laos*, an inclusive concept involving the entire fellowship of believers, was displaced. The result was a "church of the laity" and a "church of the priests." This resulted in a split-level church both theologically and experientially within the Christian household. This designation of "clergy" and "laity" will probably always be with us, but it is essential that we do not accept this division as our norm. The need today is to reassert with freshness and vigor the parity of ministry within the total household of God.

The Reformation sought to heal this false dichotomy in the church's fellowship with a rediscovery of the priesthood of all believers. The implementation of this belief has not been widely realized or practiced by the majority of Christians to the present day. The church continues to be largely subject to clericalism.

During the course of the church's history this essential biblical concept of the priesthood of all believers was submerged under layers of lethargy. The fact that there cannot be inactive members in the life of the church was overlooked. One of the real paradoxes resulting from this neglect is that laity are called to be priests but their priest-hood is denied by threatened clergy. There are excep-tions; for example, laity can celebrate the Sacraments at extraordinary times, but for the most part, the Sacraments remain the exclusive domain of the clergy. Normally, laity are trusted with counting money after the service and preparing for potluck meals at church. These are the pseudosacraments in the church's life. Even the diacon-ate, the paraprofessionals of the church, know the frustrat-ing limitations of their priesthood vis-à-vis the clergy. Will this dichotomy within the body of Christ continue in the future?

The clergy, I believe, are desirous of pursuing a respon-sible ministry. The laity wish also to be responsible co-workers. How can a meaningful duality of leadership be achieved without either party feeling displaced or threat-ened? This will continue to concern pastors in the future.

Will the clergy need to vanish, if the priesthood of all believers is to become an actuality? This question is hid-den in the thoughts of clergy and surfaces from time to time. Personally, I do not think so; everyone's talent and time have been called into service through baptism. This event is common to all believers. Our vocation (calling) through baptism is to be identified actively with the body of Christ. Through our baptism we are called into a single priesthood. This is our common stewardship; pastors will need to work out the implications of this stewardship within the life of their ministry. Every believer in some appropriate way is to exercise ministry, that is, *diakonia.* We must see ourselves as the body of Christ wherever we are employed or involved. To have this basic perception in whatever we are doing is to approximate the meaning of vocation or calling under God.

Every believer has a calling; it is not a matter exclusively reserved for the clergy. Laity as well as clergy must see the concept of the call as belonging to the entire household of faith. Neglect of this emphasis would further contribute to the dichotomized nature of the church.[2] Believers should regard their fields of endeavor (homemaking, law, retailing, teaching, carpentering, plumbing, medicine, etc.) as their stewardship, their calling, under God. Such a sublime attitude will put an entirely new framework upon our present tasks. It will certainly challenge the compromised ethics we often feel forced to practice in our jobs. In short, we will begin to appreciate with a new sense of freshness that we are a family of believers who have been called to a diversity of duties and opportunities depending upon our gifts and circumstances, but that we are ultimately all responsible to God, who has endowed each of us in a special way (I Corinthians 12). The task of the church is to help each person to understand the special way that God has called. Herein lies our oneness—we are all stewards called through our common baptism. It is within this very context that pastors should understand their sense of calling.

The pastor who can communicate through ministry this understanding of the call will, as the grass-roots theologian within the community, serve as a vital catalyst of the Spirit in helping others to understand their calling as well. We all have a responsibility of stewardship before God. This involves us all as servants before God. Servanthood is not limited to the clergy. The burden and glory of servanthood belong to each person's calling. It is in this unifying sense that we can speak meaningfully of the priesthood of all believers. Under this common mandate of stewardship and servanthood, the priesthood of all believers not only will become a living actuality, but we will begin to see the present nonsense of our division. Neither clergy nor laity will vanish in the future—each is an essential organ to the body of Christ.

Within this common priesthood and fellowship, there will come times when God's call will prompt individuals to change roles as part of their unfolding pilgrimage. No call from God is fixed for all time. It is under constant review through prayerful dialogue. What is fixed is our sense of stewardship before God, which has priority over our present involvements and careers. God can call us *from* a particular task or position as much as call us *into* a particular task or career. Our stewardship before God is a dynamic affair, not static. Our baptism has called us to responsible stewardship before God; it does not imply a locked-in feeling to our present involvements or careers. To be locked in to our respective careers is to turn deaf ears to the living God, who will always beckon us onward into the unknown. This unknown is linked to the factor of our own personal growth and self-understanding, channels through which God calls us from one task to another. The individual believer in dialogue with the community of faith must determine the nature and direction of God's dynamic calling. Each person must also aid others in fulfilling a responsible stewardship before God. Members of the household of faith need to remind each other that we are pilgrims, whose security is not found in comfortable niches we have carved out for ourselves.

Pastor and People as Pilgrims

Have the people of God today lost their identity as pilgrims? Is that why we are standing still and losing ground at the same time? The pastor is faced with these questions as the congregation begins to understand what it means to be a pilgrim. The word "pilgrim" has a distinctly noncontemporary ring. Yet a rediscovery of the implications of our pilgrimage will bring us to the door of vision, where a greater mission lies before us. To be a pilgrim is to be sensitive to God's grace rather than to our common sense. The common sense of our age invites us to play it safe. This "safe" attitude prevails in the pulpit and the pew in today's church.

It appears that today's believer is more in search of comfort than adventure. We view our faith as a cautious life insurance policy. It is almost as if our faith has become security-centered rather than Christ-centered. As a result, our actions illustrate a sense of withdrawal, a lack of creativity, daring, and boldness. If we are to take the model of the pilgrim church seriously as the people of God, "then we must expect the Church to have hazards and upsets on its journey. We must expect it to be travel-stained, flawed, weary, encumbered with much bric-a-brac and yet trying to travel lightly, forever picking itself up and starting again."[3] Do we have this vision of the church when we speak of its pilgrim nature? We must realize that the full reality of the church has not yet been realized. We are living in the anticipation of the Kingdom, not the Kingdom itself. The realization of our vision will be a "gift of God at the end of time, not something that will come about next week or in the next decade or even in the fateful year 2000."[4] This is what a pilgrim people must bear in mind.

On a more personal level, Christian growth must also be seen as a pilgrimage that engages pastor and people. The Christian life is a matter of continued growth. Christians are not to evade the challenges, struggles, difficulties, and dangers of life, but to confront and deal with them. Such challenges imply growth. Hence the pilgrim is willing to disregard "vulnerability and to venture out, even at the risk of making mistakes, for the sake of growth. This understanding of life finds expression in the figure of the Christian as wayfarer *(viator)* or pilgrim; Christian conversion is thus not, as in the mystery religions, an immediate entrance into a safe harbor but rather, though its direction has been established, the beginning of a voyage into the unknown."[5] Thus the Christian life is a movement with a direction that implies progress, "but a progress that remains incomplete in this life. The 'other-worldliness' of Christianity is significant, in this context, as the basis of the open-endedness of both personal and social development."[6] Hence, from this perspective, the worst state of a man or a woman is not so much sinfulness (for sins can be forgiven), but rather the cessation of growth, arrested development, remaining fixed at any point in life. Perhaps this lack of growth is our most serious sin as the people of God. This may be why the apostle Paul was so insistent upon comparing the Christian style of life to the discipline of running a race, for the sake of Christ (I Cor. 9:24–27). Christian immaturity is seen, then, when we refuse to grow, "the inability to cope with an open and indeterminate future (that is, the future itself), in effect the rejection of life as a process."[7] Pilgrimage is the believer's way of reaching for maturity.

Unfortunately, we seem to be unwilling to take the responsible risk of pilgrimage essential to our growth and maturity. Perhaps we too are standing with that young man who came to Jesus and said, "Sir, I will follow you wherever you go," and Jesus, perceiving the shallowness of this man's claim, challenged him by saying: "Will you really? Don't you know, that even foxes have holes and birds of the air have nests, but the Son of man hasn't a place to sleep?" (Luke 9:58). Most of us are aware that foxes have holes and that birds of the air have nests, and in the same manner we also wish to guarantee for ourselves a place to rest.

The tragedy is that we find ourselves in a situation similar to that of the Israelites during their captivity in Egypt. Unwilling to follow Moses, the Israelites were hesitant pilgrims before venturing into the wilderness toward the Promised Land. For some forty years the Israelites circled in the wilderness, going through cycles of belief and disbelief. In the wilderness they feared that even their God was dead, and so a golden calf was set up. Finally, after wandering for so many years, their new leader, Joshua, reminded them once again, on the threshold of entering the Promised Land, of the need for unswerving commitment: "Choose this day whom you will serve" (Josh. 24:15). Hesitant pilgrims, the challenge is still ours; we can't play it safe and confess to follow the biblical God in the same breath.

As hesitant pilgrims we are like the two other men who came up to Jesus desiring to follow him, until he placed a challenge before them (Luke 9:59–62). One wanted to go first and bury his father, and the other wanted to say farewell to those at home. Both requests seemed reasonable enough; however, Jesus realized that both men, through their requests, were gravitating back to the familiar in life, to the security of "home, sweet home." The men did not want to go on a pilgrimage, they simply wanted to take a tour with Jesus. These men were more concerned with home than with discipleship. Isn't this our commonsense outlook today as well? Their intention was to tour with Jesus, not commence on a pilgrimage.

There is a difference, you know, between a pilgrim and a tourist. Today's affluency has produced many tourists. A tourist is one who sets out with a more or less fixed itinerary, scheduled to get back after so many days, eager and ready to show souvenirs to friends and relatives. In fact, tourists abroad are often so anxious to get back that they find hamburger and hot-dog stands to remind them of home. At last, after several weeks the tourist returns with Samsonite luggage in hand and a camera strapped over the shoulder, tired but glad to be home.

A pilgrim, from the biblical perspective, has no fixed itinerary. The pilgrim sets out, making stops under orders from God, not looking back to the security of home. The pilgrim, possessing eyes of faith, knows that there is no abiding home here, only the promise that God will go with us wherever we may be. The trouble for many pastors and parishioners is that we have looked at the matter of commitment from the standpoint of a tourist rather than as a pilgrim.

Some, in fact, think it is only the business of ministers and missionaries to live committed lives. G. K. Chesterton, British writer, hinted at this false conclusion in his statement, "People pay ministers to be good, to show the rest of us it doesn't pay to be good." Fortunately, facts prove otherwise. The biblical witness is clear, we are all called into discipleship. The call to be a follower of Christ is universal and inclusive. Yet only a few see themselves as pilgrims, while the majority of us have a settler's mentality. A pilgrim from the viewpoint of the majority is a fanatic, and who among us wants that label? Yet the obvious fact is that many of us have already become fanatics in our search for other goals outside of Christ. As a result, we have become hesitant pilgrims as Christians. The church as a consequence is filled with hesitant pilgrims suffering from an identity crisis.

The Lord of the church hasn't limited his call to ministers and missionaries, but has extended it to everyone who willingly claims to be a follower of Christ. At times our ambiguous thinking confuses our careers and our Christian calling. There are many careers to which we feel drawn, depending upon our abilities, circumstances, and tastes, but there is only one calling for every Christian and that is to be a witness for Jesus Christ. This is our common stewardship, to be executed through our respective careers and involvements. There should be no confusion at this point. To be baptized in the name of Christ is to be identified with the mission of Christ; it means taking your place in an elite corps that knows no end of service or servanthood.

Of course, to follow Jesus may mean leaving familiar faces and situations, an insecure future from the world's commonsense standpoint. Are we still willing to follow him? To follow him is to follow him on his terms. Most of us wish to follow him on our terms. The world says, the family says, even we say, "Play it safe." But an attempt to follow him can be anything but safe![8] Not long ago, a concerned mother and father who were very active in church asked me about their son's desire to invest a few years of his life in the work of the church. The son was an engineer and wanted to serve in some related capacity for the church, either at home or overseas. However, the parents had reservations about their son going off to some "godforsaken place," not to mention the fact that he would be leaving behind a well-paying job. The son's desire to volunteer his service was not really the commonsense approach. Following Jesus often involves doing the uncommon thing.

In the book of Revelation we read about the Christians in the church at Laodicea (Rev. 3:14–16). What do we discover about these Christians? They were neither hot nor cold about their commitment to Christ, but simply lukewarm. This implies a diluted commitment, which is another way of playing it safe. Christ says to the church filled with lukewarm members, "I wish you were either hot or cold, but not lukewarm." From the standpoint of God, lukewarmness is worse than outright coldness; lukewarmness is diluted commitment. How different from our commonsense attitude! There is really no such thing as halfhearted commitment.

Where do we stand today? Only an unconditional commitment to Christ will prove fulfilling in our lives. Are we victimized today by the status quo, comfort, or fear? Is it our intention to serve him as tourists or as pilgrims? Only as pastor and people together become more than hesitant pilgrims can the Christian church hope to emerge from its present identity crisis and reassert itself as a house of vision in tomorrow's world. To do so, the laity must become co-pastors with the clergy.

Laity as Co-Pastors

Recently a neighbor offered me a ride from the airport, along with two of his colleagues. After we were all settled in the car and on our way, introductions began. My neighbor, a Presbyterian layman, presented me as a Presbyterian minister teaching in a seminary. "Is that right?" remarked one of the guests. "Why, I am a Presbyterian, too." "You don't say, Bob," replied my neighbor. "In our years of association, I had wondered what your religion was." The next few seconds we rode on in silence. The second gentleman, who as yet hadn't spoken, broke the silence with, "You know, boys, I'm a Presbyterian, too." This gentleman happened to be the senior officer of the firm, and the others' surprise that their boss was a member of the same "club" was an obvious fact of delight. By the time we reached home, it was apparent that we had gained a closer bond of identification with one another.

Later my neighbor was visiting me and we recalled the incident of the previous week. In our mutual reflections, we came up with the following observations, which may well reflect the outlook of many Protestant, Catholic, and Orthodox church people today:

Whether the pastor wishes to admit it or not, there exist for a majority of Christians two realms—namely, the career world and the churchly world. Among associates in places of business, the laity do not express their churchmanship; this is evidently an area of conversation to be avoided, regardless of the exhortations of pastors on Sundays. In practice, most laity limit their religious affiliations to the domestic areas of their lives. Their primary "mission" during the week is to earn the "bread and butter"

for the family and to help maintain the church as a charac-
ter-building institution for their children and as an activity
center for the women.

Pastors' sermons, according to the filter system of the
typical laity, are primarily aimed toward the good of children. Yet the number of young people who find the
church meaningful is decreasing. Nevertheless, the traditional laity believe the church plays its part toward a bal-
anced life as an extracurricular activity. At best, the lay
population of the church consider themselves "weekend
assistants" to the local pastor. They assist the pastor in the
"secondary" aspects of worship and organization, often
performing the "dry run" rather than the real event.
These weekend assistants, sometimes referred to as "spark
plugs" in the congregation, are generally in short supply,
as most pastors will readily testify.

Tension rises in the church when the "spark plug" layperson becomes overzealous and appears to challenge the
pastor's judgments. What's really expected in the normal
life of the church is for the ordained and the nonordained
to act their respective roles and in addition to laugh together, attend church suppers, and exchange sweet noth-
ings following the Sunday service. The result has been, for
Protestants as well as for Catholics and Orthodox, the
emergence of two ghettos—a ghetto of the laity and a
ghetto of the clergy—with little authentic conversation
between them.

Both ghettos are in need of cleansing and purification:
The world is in the church as much as the church is in the
world. We have talked too long about taking the church
to the world, while actually on any given Sunday the world
comes to the church. Here is one of the greatest missionary frontiers: to destroy the false barriers that continually
divide "church and world" as two entities set off from each
other. These two realms are within each other, and together form the reality of God's creation.

The ride from the airport revealed the dual existence, *the private and public levels,* which the laity maintain, often through the help of insensitive clergy. The result has been a *split-level church* for our laity, where the pastor is considered the professional alter ego of the laity. This split behavior in private and public life is commonly accepted without serious question as a necessary right for survival in "the secular city." Before we acquiesce to the presence of this secularized duality, let us examine the cost of the resulting fragmentation and dehumanization in the laity's world.

Laypersons' public existence is geared for a "cut-throat" existence. Laity have periodic respites as they "retreat" home to recover from the wounds of the day. At home one expresses tender feelings by gardening or relaxing in play with the children. Most pastors see this "tender side" of their parishioners and orient themselves accordingly on Sunday, thereby contributing to the dilemma of duality. In fact, the "discriminating pastor" knows that the parishioner desires some kind words to nurture this private world and even to disregard the public side of life. This is at times erroneously interpreted as a need to place emphasis upon the "spiritual" side of ministry. More often than not, the clergy comply with these wishes.

What happens to the church at this point? It responds to the expectations of the laity by becoming a "fellowship center." The church becomes an extended "family room," keeping retired persons and children busy while most working moms and dads are busy or resting at home. In this setting the pastor is subtly transformed into a domestic accessory to help tidy up the "family room," but above all to leave the family's business affairs alone! For what does the pastor know about putting "bread and butter" on the table? One irate contractor complained to me in Los Angeles during a period of racial tensions: "Listen, preachers are paid to keep their hands clean. . . . They have no business stirring up blacks about their rights; their job is to save souls. That's the only business they know!" The cautious clergy, with this warning in mind, will direct their comments to support the restful atmosphere of country life.

Much Christian worship, in effect, is designed to accommodate the above outlook. The result is worship of a *spiritualized incarnation,* directed solely toward "soul-saving," which is incomplete without a social dimension. However, a *materialized incarnation* concentrated on social concern without a note of personal redemption is also incomplete. Worship of the incarnate one involves both the personal and the social, the spiritual and the material, fused together into a sacramental whole. Any reduction of this wholeness is heresy, just as any splitting of the incarnation is a loss of its mystery and glory. This duality practiced in Christian worship is another expression of the laity's dilemma carried into the sanctuary. This liturgical and existential dichotomy contributes to the sense of lost identity felt by countless Christians in the church today. Lost identity has contributed to a state of collective amnesia, which will not be overcome until the worshiper unites all areas of life under God.

Such a union will challenge and eventually displace the false division between private and public existence. My neighbor and his business associates will enter then upon greater opportunities to raise questions about life and death. And isn't this the meaning of Christian witness? Isn't this the vocational calling of every layperson? When will the laity see themselves as co-pastors with clergy in fulfilling their vocational obligation, which is the task of every believer? The responsibility lies equally with clergy and laity to make a shift in their present perception of themselves. What are the prospects for such a shift?

Hope lies, it seems to me, at the level of *personal encounter.* The priesthood of all believers, advanced by Protestants, Catholics, and Orthodox, has been and will continue to be no more than a *paper theology* unless my neighbor and his business associates are willing to be incarnate witnesses at work and at play. Unless the homemaker and the breadwinner are willing to expose themselves and their faith in some tangible way, there is little hope that the priesthood of all believers will become anything more than a *paper theology*.

Mission is not simply a programmed and systematic enterprise carried on by the institutional church. Mission depends upon persons. Mission begins whenever and wherever individuals take it upon themselves to raise questions of life and death with their neighbors in the name of Jesus Christ. Frankly, this implies overcoming the gap that currently exists between private and public existence. It happens when clergy invite laity to truly serve with them as co-pastors.

How can this be brought about? Only through a shift from a *paper theology* to a *practicing theology* of the priesthood of all believers. This will happen when the laity truly see themselves as the people *(laos)* of God. One layman shared with my class of seminarians the opinion that "the church is really too important to be trusted only to the professional clergy." The clergy historically, either through domination or through default of the laity, have contributed to the church's split-level existence. Neither clericalism nor laicism is desirable, and each is contrary to the spirit of *laos*. The laity must recognize themselves as ministers ordained in their baptism to a life of witness, whatever their secular occupation. Pastors must consider themselves as baptized laity ordained to be the grass-roots theologians within the life and mission of the church which belongs to the whole people *(laos)* of God. As a team, clergy and laity can enjoy an atmosphere of interdependence under the guidance of the Holy Spirit, who points us to the living God.

Gone are the days, it is hoped, when "missionaries" or "pastors" alone are held responsible for maintaining a Christian witness. The *laos* concept, rightly applied, has no room for "second-class Christians." All baptized Christians are "called" and committed to consecrate "their world" to the Creator. Hence the church's renewal depends upon everyone's becoming a chaplain, a priest to neighbors at home, at the factory, at school, in business, or wherever time is spent each day. Many churches are trying to suggest this emphasis on the front page of their Sunday bulletin under the heading, "MINISTERS: ALL THE MEMBERS OF THIS CHURCH."

The vital church will find its membership serving as co-pastors to each other and to the larger community where they live and work. Only as we move together as one team—as the people of God—can the church have any hope of enhancing its mission in the world. The danger at this point is to state glibly that *laity must be seen as pastors, and clergy must be seen as laity;* there is wide wasteland between this ideal and the actual. However, only as laity and clergy begin gradually to learn, receive, and listen on the one hand and to teach, share, and confess on the other can they hope to realize their potential as the people of God, becoming a dynamic organism under the guidance of the Spirit.

Difficult questions still remain before us: Can we go beyond our present categories of division, where the clergy are expected to be preoccupied with "spiritual functions" and the laity with "secular functions"? Can we be spiritual without being secular or secular without being spiritual? Will our piety enable us to see Jesus Christ as *the layperson,* worshiped by clergy and laity alike as example and Lord? If baptism in the name of *this layperson* gives the laity equal citizenship with the clergy in the life of the church, what implications will that have for future structuring of the church? The answers to these questions call for an ecumenically corporate endeavor; and the resources of all the members are certainly needed if the pastor is to benefit fully from the leadership of the laity.

If the leadership of the laity is to be truly realized, pastors will need to give careful attention to the following steps:

ONE: *A higher grade of theological education should be provided for the laity.* Effective collegiality in ministry depends upon greater depth in nurture as well as opportunities for service. Laity who are better educated theologically will be supportive to the pastor who wishes to function as the community's grass-roots theologian. One of the ways to achieve this theological education is to utilize more effectively theological seminaries and educational centers throughout the country. Many seminaries are involved in aspects of lay education, but how many theological seminaries have structured into their program a place for the laity as a part of their total enterprise? How many seminaries provide scholarships and other forms of encouragement to the laity? If we are really one church through baptism, why should financial aid and scholarships be limited to ministerial candidates? The presence of laity for a semester or year's program not only will be of benefit to them but also will enhance the quality of dialogue within our seminaries as we wrestle together on the implications of the priesthood of all believers for the pastor and the laity.

TWO: *Pastors should have as a guiding motto never to do a task for which a layperson is better qualified.* Such a motto may prove threatening to clergy, but it is the best way to ensure common ownership in the church. Involvement requires participation; and participation is often prevented when clergy usurp the job of the laity. If the above motto is maintained, not only will laity be encouraged to get involved, but also laity will ask what it is that their pastor should be about. "What is the primary task of the pastor?" should always be a major question before the laity. To neglect this question will tend to leave the leadership of the laity underdeveloped, and will also find the pastor performing as an amateur at tasks he or she has never been trained or called on to perform. Laity are the general practitioners of the parish; the clergy are called to be theological specialists—the grass-roots theologians within the community. When pastors neglect this motto, they feel compelled to attempt everything and thus become master of nothing. The temptation for pastors is to subvert this motto for what might appear to be good reasons, but which in the long run will rob the church of its vitality.

THREE: *Pastors who wish to avoid the pitfalls of being either a superstar or a fallen messiah within their parish should educate the congregation from the beginning that the church belongs to the people.* The clergy minister on behalf of the church, but ministry belongs to the church. The pastor who understands this will lead from the middle, living in the midst of the people, providing the climate in which lay leadership can be nurtured and expressed. The usual expectation is for pastors to lead from the front, developing into a "one-man show" to the detriment of the congregation's growth. Pastors must be confident in their own self-understanding, to avoid the temptations and pressures of superficial prominence. People will respect pastors whose leadership profile is low and whose style is inclusive, involving many persons in leadership roles.

FOUR: *Pastors, who are attuned to the needs of the marketplace, will encourage qualified persons among the laity to minister meaningfully to those needs.* Matching proper talent to societal needs is more effective than most churchly pronouncements. The involvement of knowledgeable lay leadership will place the church on the frontiers of ministry and will develop supportive laity to share the pastor's concerns and compassion.

As these above steps are taken, the clergy will see greatness developing within the laity—the awakening of neglected power—that will surpass all expectation. The future depends upon the laity to implement their role as co-pastors with today's clergy.

Let us now consider the material realities of life, an area often slighted by the clergy.

5
The Material Side
of Ministry

Pastors are Christian materialists. That is to say, pastors
need to understand clearly that the material and spiritual
dimensions of life are integrally related. The material is
spiritual and the spiritual is material; they are organically
united in life. This is why we are able to say that the daily
bread we eat represents the sacramental nature of our
world. Bread is both spiritual and material. Equipped with
this basic theological premise, pastors minister to others,
often translating concerns and compassion tangibly
through material assistance. This is why we take offerings
in our churches and convert these monetary funds into
material means of ministry at home and abroad. A portion
of the offerings is used for the care and maintenance of the
clergy. Tomorrow's clergy and laity will need to take a
more serious look at the standards of care and maintenance for the pastor. This material side of ministry has
become a more acute issue since (1) the expectations of
clergy have risen, while membership has declined, (2) rising costs and inflation in our culture are realities, and (3)
the pastor's ambition and career goals vary within a lifetime.

Employment Possibilities in the Future

When I became an ordained pastor in 1958 there was a shortage of clergy, and church membership was growing. The possibility never troubled me that there might be difficulty in finding employment in a parish. In fact, most of my classmates that year faced the problem of which available opportunity to choose. In retrospect, we know that from 1945 to 1965, membership in Protestant churches soared from 43 million to about 69 million. Since 1965, church membership for many major denominations has decreased, and the previous scarcity of pastors has become a surplus. This surplus varies from denomination to denomination; there are some churches that continue to have acute pastoral shortages, due to various factors. This is true for the Catholic Church, which has lost a number of priests in the years since Vatican II.

Pastors planning to serve in one of the major Protestant denominations within the near future will have limited employment possibilities. Several denominational leaders regard the surplus to be temporary and expect a return to shortages by the mid-'80s. Those who predict a continuing shortage suggest closing or merging existing seminaries or declaring a moratorium on ministerial candidates for several years. President James I. McCord, of Princeton Theological Seminary, in his presidential letter to alumni, searches for a meaningful explanation of the recent increase in seminary enrollment while church membership continues to decline. He writes:

How does one understand the paradox of declining church membership and increased enrollment in the seminaries? In part, the increase is due to more able and committed young women entering seminary. Another factor is the reawakened interest in the faith and ministry on the part of this student generation. I have remarked before that historically a rise in the number of ministerial candidates generally precedes a renascence in the Church and a fresh movement outward in witness and evangelism. There is no reason why our Church cannot be turned around and begin to grow, form new congregations and capture for Jesus Christ the thousands who are seeking a way amidst the vulgarities of today's society.[1]

I would like to share McCord's perspective, but, for the immediate future, pastors and graduating seminarians can expect to experience difficulty in finding placement in parishes that are economically feasible. There is, of course, the usual rationalization that there will always be places for *good* men and women in the parish. I believe this, but the designation *good* is discounted, especially when limited opportunities are sometimes distributed through apparent "patronage" rather than ability. *A major factor facing today's and tomorrow's pastor will be the question of supply and demand.* (This issue is not limited to the professional ministry; it is faced by individuals in other professions as well.) To what extent should churches maintain a responsible control over supply and demand? Is such control really impossible to maintain and even distasteful, given the evangelical concerns of the church? These are a few questions that clergy and laity must ask themselves *now.*

I would like to suggest some realistic options for tomorrow's clergy and laity, to enhance the church's witness in the world while concurrently improving employment possibilities. They are the following:

ONE: *The churches can be more selective in the quality of candidates for future ministry.* Churches should not depend upon seminaries to be the chief agents in this selection process. Actually, seminaries seek students in order to stay in business. The severity of the selection process must begin with the ecclesiastical body that recommends the student to ministry. This will maintain grass-roots control in the matter and encourage seminaries to work more closely with the churches. The seminary is always at liberty, of course, to admit additional students who do not have ecclesiastical sponsorship, but if churches are responsible for the ordination and licensing process, they should also be concerned with the supply and demand balance. Church committees, it is hoped, will be less timid and more realistic in their selection process. Seminaries do not perform miracles; the basic talents of the candidate often are established before the person enters the seminary. If laity desire greatness in their clergy, then they must initiate the process by choosing amoung possible candidates only those who show a promise of greatness. We have too often refrained from criticism as we look for the Spirit's leading; as a result, we have become too ambiguous and accepting in our judgments. Later, then, this kind acceptance turns to bitter contempt when the candidate becomes a pastor and does not live up to our fantasized expectations. We have done a disservice not only to the church but to the individual involved. Careful screening is part of our stewardship in the household of faith, if we truly believe that the church belongs to the people of God.

TWO: *The average term of seminary education should be extended from three years to four.* Lutheran seminaries already require four years. In a time of surplus, theological seminaries, as servants of the churches, have a responsible task to upgrade the quality of theological education. Protestant seminarians tend to be in too great a hurry to complete their theological education in the shortest possible time. This is due to financial considerations often, but in our hurriedness we are not adequately preparing our candidates academically or spiritually. If incoming candidates knew that theological education required four vigorous years, they might hesitate to make that kind of commitment. (The length of medical education causes many to turn to other vocations.) A long period of training will not only enhance the quality of leadership, but it will also slow the process of preparing more graduates than churches can realistically accommodate. This will help ease the immediate tension and, at the same time, be a benefit both to individual candidates in training and to the church-at-large.

A lengthened seminary education should also enable the qualified graduate to earn a Doctor of Ministry degree. The present Master of Divinity degree, issued by nearly all accredited seminaries, will eventually evolve, I believe, into a Doctor of Ministry degree comparable to the fields of medicine and law. Some of the hopeful consequences would be a better qualified pastor and also the elimination of the "doctoral degree game" among pastors who are tempted to secure easy doctorates through mail order and unaccredited institutions. It would also create a healthy class of paraprofessionals who want to serve in some form of ministry but do not want the responsibilities associated with a Doctor of Ministry degree. At present, the Master of Religious Education or Master of Arts in Religion for paraprofessionals is not sufficiently distinguishable from the Master of Divinity degree for potential pastors.

THREE: *Practicing pastors should be encouraged to return to a year or more of additional education to refresh their theological methods and also to earn a Doctor of Ministry degree.* This would strengthen the continuing education program within churches and provide incentive for many pastors whose present continuing education is a "hit-or-miss" proposition. This move will encourage some pastors to accumulate three or more months of study leave time for a meaningful educational sabbatical from the parish. Churches with such a program for clergy will not only enrich themselves, they will also provide new employment opportunities. Supplying replacements for pastors who are on sabbatical leaves can also provide an early retirement policy that will enable a pastor to leave a permanent parish and have continued ministry in a temporary situation. The congregation will benefit from this new exposure without losing the meaningful relationship with their pastor on sabbatical. A program of sabbatical leaves and early retirement should be coordinated at the national level by each denomination. With early retirement made more attractive, employment possibilities for the younger pastor will increase.

FOUR: *Looking to the future, churches must ascertain what areas in the marketplace need special attention and trained personnel.* There will be an increasing demand for family counselors, ministry to the elderly, and youth specialists from the ranks of today's pastors. Setting aside funds for this purpose will guarantee and encourage these pastoral positions in communities where local resources are limited. A national endowment within each denomination, where funds and personnel can be deployed, will create meaningful employment for a number of pastors. Affluent congregations will have a special responsibility to contribute to this national endowment dedicated to meeting the needs in small towns and rural areas as well as in urban situations. Other specialized ministries will also evolve in the future, as realistic studies are made of life-styles and their implications. The pastor who understands these trends and becomes appropriately trained not only will find employment but will bring a theological awareness to these newly acquired skills that will make the church more responsible and responsive to the marketplace.

FIVE: *There will always be opportunities for employment and ministry for those pastors who are willing to maintain a tentmaking ministry.* Pastors who can financially support themselves independently of the congregation will also find opportunities for ministry. It is not easy to hold two jobs; there is often the danger that neither is done well or that one becomes subordinated to the other. Whatever the case, tentmaking ministries have a biblical precedent and will increase in the future. The pastor who contemplates this option seriously should begin now to acquire the necessary secular proficiencies to accompany theological skills. For instance, Pittsburgh Theological Seminary already has joint degree programs with the University of Pittsburgh for this purpose.

These above suggestions are some possibilities to ease the current surplus of pastors and to provide more opportunities for meaningful employment. It is my own conviction that there will always be a great need in the marketplace for the sensitive and alert pastor who can confront persons in creative and imaginative ways. The pastor can be assured that society will always be searching for purpose and meaning. The pastor who can give meaningful direction will always find useful employment. The financial support of these pastors will be subject to wise planning and faith.

Realities in a Business Culture

Faith and wise planning must be partners in our churches. Faith without planning will often leave churches in a state of panic. This panic is a dehumanizing process that has victimized many servants of God. Wise planning depends upon recognizing the realities of our business culture. The pastor cannot avoid the implications of rising cost, inflation, and demands for a living wage. There are still those who contend that these are not the concerns of a "servant." It is my observation that most clergy I know, including celibates, do not interpret servanthood as a restriction to live on the lower end of the economic spectrum. Most clergy in America, for better or worse, are conditioned to a middle-class median of existence. Pastors with families especially want to provide adequate housing and education for their children. And everything costs money!

By the same token, the poor in an affluent nation like ours are getting poorer. Who, other than a celibate, can afford to minister for long to the poor, if the opportunities and living conditions for the pastor's family are deteriorating? As a consequence, clergy, like their colleagues in other fields, tend to gravitate to middle-class communities with affluency, adequate school systems, community responsibility, and so forth. This is where most of us are, isn't it? We would like to think otherwise in our rhetoric and pious declarations, but the fact is that we are Christian materialists and differ only in degree from the wealthy and upper middle class in the number of possessions and privileges that money and status buy. This is all a part of our culture; I do not believe today's pastor can escape it.

How, then, is the pastor to develop a viable posture vis-à-vis these realities? How is the pastor to be any more than a hired hand of middle-class America? This question has not been answered by today's clergy, and it is questionable if the future pastor will be able to do better. Of course, we all know and believe that pastors are not hired hands. They have a divine task in a local community—to be grass-roots theologians among the people of God. But how free are pastors to perform this function? One pastor confided in me, after nearly twenty years of ministry, that the only truly prophetic pastor is the one who has a million dollars in the bank. "Pastors with a million dollars can afford to speak their mind." Would you accept this conclusion? How many pastors in the 1960s did speak their minds and then watched their careers and families suffer? The current mood is one of more caution regarding our prophetic role; the decade of the '60s is still too freshly implanted in our minds. Are we then willing to agree with the cynic who observed, "So long as the preachers are well fed, they give their blessing to the status quo." Is this also a reality of our culture that the pastor must keep in mind?

Most of us want pastors to be more than puppets. Yet, given the economics of life, congregations clearly remind their pastors in subtle (and not so subtle) ways of the source of clergy salaries. Churches have experienced economic boycotts on the local and national levels when parishioners are unhappy with church policy or prophetic utterances. Our situation today is really no different from that of the early Reformers. "A Swiss layman at Neuchatel said to William Farel in 1541, 'I fire a servant who displeases me, why not a pastor?' And some congregations have stooped so low as to deliberately 'starve out' their minister. Fortunately such a vicious attitude is rare. Basically the pulpit is free."[2] The question for today's pastor is how to maintain the freedom of the pulpit in a responsible way before God and the congregation.

The grass-roots theologian knows that one's first loyalty is to God; pastors are not duty-bound to preach what the congregation wishes to hear. In practice, this is difficult to discern, since the rationalizing process to avoid offense is a subtle force of great power. As a result, the ministry has come to depend more and more on public goodwill, even more than on competence. Admittedly, public goodwill and competence are necessary in all professions. Doctors have to satisfy their patients, but they set their own office hours and write their own prescriptions. Lawyers must satisfy their clients, but they determine their own fees. Ministers seem to have hardly a voice in controlling their profession, although this varies from denomination to denomination. In practice, however, it seems that pastors become what people want them to be, the sum of the things they are asked to be. If any pastor defies these expectations, the realities of our business culture threaten the very ground of his or her existence. As a result, it seems no other professional is quite so eager to please as the pastor. Consequently, the pastor has exchanged the ethics of the profession for an inoffensive etiquette. For instance, "Let's check on our telephone habits," suggests a minister's handbook. "Do you answer the telephone before the third ring?"[3] Has the professional backbone of today's pastor been jeopardized beyond correction? Will the pastor be able to do better in the future?

To face the realities of our business culture, pastors will be subject to numerous cross fires and will be vulnerable at some time or another, if being a responsible professional in ministry. It takes strong people to seek the pastoral office; this has always been the case. Some abuse of one's office or person can be expected.

To minimize the abuse and to avoid suffering in vain, the pastor will need to establish rapport with the congregation on several points that involve material consideration. First, pastors must develop an understanding of their own self-worth and then test it out among peers. People do not receive what they are worth unless they first have some idea of their worth. This is a fact within our economic society. The actual price paid will depend also upon the supply-and-demand factor at the time. Yet, in another sense, all pastors have inner wealth if they have confidence and confirmation of their worth. This can be the pastor's million dollars in the bank.

Second, pastors must be able to communicate this self-worth to congregations interested in their services. This communication is facilitated if the denomination has studied the matter and provided some guidelines.[4] Communication implies a frankness on the part of the pastor in negotiating with the congregation or its committee. False modesty is to be shunned. Some laypersons, it is hoped, will be empathetic and realistic on behalf of the pastor's needs. The pastor may wish, in addition, to receive training in negotiation skills, since speaking for oneself is not easy. Failure to speak up, however, often leads to personal budget difficulties. It causes some pastors to appear devious as they try to negotiate around the congregation or the committee at a later date. It is really a matter of stewardship to be able to speak up at the appropriate time.

Third, the congregation has a right to expect a measure of accountability for the services rendered. This may call for an agreement or contract between the pastor and the congregation. This provision is provided for in some denominational structures. Accountability really involves a code of ethics between the pastor and the people, which ought to confront the realities and expectations of both parties who together are part of the same business culture. It should be a dynamic instrument, providing for review and revision on a regular basis. Outstanding performance by the pastor should be acknowledged and provided for by guidelines agreed upon by the pastor and the congregation. Showing tangible appreciation is one of the important realities within our business culture. The pastor likewise must remember to show appreciation to the congregation.

Fourth, since congregations are made up of persons, there will be in the life of any healthy congregation honest differences of opinion and smoldering conflicts. This, too, is another reality of our business culture that needs to be faced. How a pastor manages conflict will be a test of one's worth. The pastor who develops skills in conflict management and steers clear of any superficial application of reconciliation will be a valuable person in the life of that congregation. He or she is worthy of a handsome compensation if a church is saved from further splitting and fragmentation. At times, there are doctrinal issues in the life of the church that lead to splits, but more often such "doctrinal issues" are underlying personality or power conflicts within the church. The pastor who shows leadership at such points and restores wholeness by the grace of God is certainly of value to the congregation and should be generously rewarded. Saving the life of a congregation can be as meaningful as saving the life of an individual through proper medical care.

Fifth, the pastor whose ministry shows a well-balanced competency is in the best position to practice a prophetic ministry to the congregation and the community. This often requires many years, in which one gains the right to be heard on the controversial issues of the day. To be silent on the issues is to demote the significance of one's ministry. How and when one speaks are key issues in exercising an effective ministry prophetically. The pastor who seeks to be a prophet without doing adequate homework and whose style of ministry does not show evident competency will only be a fool. The pastor who is both prophetically responsible and courageous will be respected, even in difficulty. Burdens will not be in vain; carrying one's cross should make a difference in the quality of life in that congregation and community. A prophetic ministry that has the greatest impact will be based upon the broadest coalition, as the pastor learns to lead from the middle. A prophetic ministry does not necessarily imply that the pastor must stand before the congregation or community. The effective pastoral leader will understand this. The pastor who is prophetically involved in broadening a congregation's concern from its own narrowly conceived self-interest may not be beloved, but the ministry is not a popularity contest. The integrity of one's ministry will always include a lively dimension of prophetic ministry.

Pastors may not always experience personal satisfaction from a prophetic ministry. In fact, the pastor may feel the need to move on to another parish because things become too stormy. This is unfortunate, since a premature move will not enable the pastor and people to grow closer together following their times of conflict. Pastors who move frequently in their ministry will not be able to exercise the depth of prophetic ministry needed in a given community. Personally, I would like to see pastors commit themselves to long-term ministries in a given place. The surplus of clergy will reduce some of the pastoral mobility known in recent years. I think this will be a good thing. Clergy have too long been identified professionally as "church tramps." This needs to stop. Let us not always be running from situations that become either "too hot" or "too boring," denying ourselves a ministry in depth in one parish. Professional growth is more possible when we are committed to a longer ministry; otherwise we are too tempted to repeat the materials of our first five years of ministry several times. In short, pastors will find that a prophetic ministry will be dependent upon the competency and length of ministry in a single community. The pastor's prophetic ministry will have the greatest impact upon the people when these two criteria are met.

Sixth and last, pastors must always bear in mind that no matter how harsh the realities of our business culture appear at times, ultimately we are all subject to the judgment and mercy of God. There is a transcendent accountability that takes precedence over the transient business culture in which our ministry takes place. We must keep this perspective before us; so often the immediate details of the present seem larger and more real than our allegiance to God. Our personal strivings and struggles will find their meaning or meaninglessness in the divine presence. Greatness in ministry cannot be measured by the adequacy or size of our compensation or rewards. Rather, it will be seen through our life-style, fulfilling, it is hoped, the radical nature of faith.

Ambition in the Ministry

In discussing the material side of ministry, we must also address ourselves to the question of ambition in ministry. Perhaps the lack of greatness in ministry is due to the lack of ambition among clergy. Is this what that business layman had in mind when he raised the question, "Can the laity expect greatness from the clergy?" Was the business layman looking for more ambition in the clergy? Certainly, we know that in our business world those without ambition will have a difficult time. Should a similar perspective be ours in ministry? How should ambition be viewed among clergy? Is it a negative goal to avoid? Is the spiritually-minded pastor above ambition? Is the aim of our pilgrimage and spiritual formation as believers to overcome ambition for a self-emptying of ourselves? Concern over ambition cannot be avoided by the pastor or by the congregation as we reach for the meaning of greatness.

Ambition is a universal trait among human beings. We normally are alarmed if our children do not show ambition. Ambition essentially implies the drive to achieve— honor, fame, career, power, wealth, rank, office, or some other goal deemed worthy by the individual and society. Ambition is an expression of human self-assertion, the desire to become someone or contribute something to society. Individuals without ambition appear dull; persons without self-assertion are nonentities. Every person will have a struggle with ambition—it may be a positive force in accomplishing goals, but it can also be a negative force that leads to frustrating moments and personal feelings of nonacceptance. None of us can escape our confrontation with ambition; it is woven into the human tapestry of our being, conditioned and reinforced in numerous ways from culture to culture. How to handle this force in ourselves and place it within theological perspective is the task of every believer—clergy and laity. We are all in need of direction and guidance in this area.

For the grass-roots theologian, ambition must be interpreted from biblical guidelines. These guidelines indicate that ambition must be seen as an integral aspect of our created nature. The story of Genesis implies not only that humankind has responsibility for the whole of created life but that God expects us to be fruitful, multiply, and cultivate the whole of creation to his glory (Gen. 1:26–31). In short, God not only unfolds to us the gift of life and its perpetuation but endows us with the drive to maintain his created order as a fulfillment of our destiny—to be his sons and daughters. When our ambition, our drive, is not designed to preserve the whole of created life, but is perverted and turned toward self-aggrandizement, then we have indeed fallen from grace. In short, we have sinned by defiling the intention and goal of our created nature. Another biblical guideline is that ambition not only reflects the intent of our created nature but also is a measurable gauge of our stewardship. We are all blessed with different abilities, but we are called upon to develop these abilities to the utmost (Matt. 25:14–30). This is not only a quantitive matter but a qualitative concern as well. We are living on borrowed time; no one's life is endless. We must reach for standards of excellence, within the limited number of years each of us has, as an expression of our stewardship. The execution of our stewardship involves ambition; which of us wishes to do less than our best as our offering before God? The final biblical guideline instructs us to reserve judgment on the ambitions, motives, and intentions of fellow believers, knowing that the final judgment of anyone's actions will be God's to determine (Eccl. 3:17). We are only in a penultimate position, therefore our opinions and rationalizations to explain our own drives and those of others will be subject to his final judgment. Knowing this, we need to live in a less judgmental frame of mind toward ourselves and others.

The pastor with these biblical guidelines must consciously nurture a *baptized ambition* among the people of God. A baptized ambition is consciously aware of the sequence of our Lord's ministry—an earthly ministry that was uninhibited and inclusive, ending with death on the cross for the sake of others and the promise of resurrection to those who believe. Baptized ambition calls us then to be stewards of this ministry through our respective careers, involvements, and when necessary with our very lives. Individually, most of us are not equal to the task; collectively as a body of believers, supporting each other in love, we have a chance to seek ambitiously to fulfill this ministry in Christ.

In a more personal way, each of us must wrestle with our own individual priorities in fulfilling this baptized ambition. Each of us must ask: "How much ambition should I personally have as a pastor? How much ambition should I personally have as a member of the *laos?*" George E. Sweazey, a pastor with a distinguished career, has written, "Clearly, ambition has no place in the Christian ministry —but the Church would be in a bad way without it."[5] Sweazey goes on to indicate the pros and cons of ambition in ministry.[6] The reasons why pastors should be ambitious are: (1) The need for achievement is common to all professions and persons; (2) ambition is necessary for the pastor's own mental health—tangible evidence of one's ministry is encouraging when so much of one's ministry is intangible; (3) ambition is a needed goal—as a self-employed individual the pastor needs some kind of pacesetter to maintain some form of discipline; and (4) the pastor's ambition is viewed as a challenge to see what can be done to improve a situation.

The negative aspects of the pastor's ambition are (1) the tendency toward self-aggrandizement and the displacement of the servant image; (2) the conflict in the pastor's life-style—a striving for success and acceptance at the expense of one's prophetic role; (3) the futile pursuit of a receding goal—the dissatisfaction that stems from reaching a superficial goal when viewed in retrospect; and (4) the depiction of the pastor as a hard-driving individual who might actually become a negative model to a tense, hard-driven people. An ambitious, hard-driving pastor may not have the time to listen to the pent-up emotions and hurts of the congregation.

Well, where does this lead our discussion on ambition in the ministry? There is certainly no clear direction; pastors without ambition seem either dull or lazy, while ambitious pastors may appear to be aggressive and self-serving. It is also true that ambition will vary with age. The phenomenal growth and interest in career counseling for pastors in recent years has brought this to the surface. Pastors in their mid-twenties often have an eagerness and desire to establish a reputation and experiment with the congregation; pastors in their thirties have tried many directions and are now settling in with a style of ministry that makes sense to them; pastors in their forties are nearing their peak in productivity and beginning the painful process of reassessment of their ministries; pastors in their fifties are beginning to eye their retirement and wondering if their present position will be their last; and pastors in their sixties are sometimes eager to retire and begin a new chapter in their lives or find it difficult to step aside for a younger colleague. Some pastors near retirement are simply worried that they will not have enough financial support, and yet realize that the "spunk" and creativity of their ministry has been spent. Ambition will certainly vary within each of these life cycles.

Not only does ambition vary with age but ambition has also been viewed in terms of winners and losers, categories of our success-oriented culture. Pastors with ambition are seen as potential winners; pastors with minimum ambition (or those who even shun it) are considered losers. An attorney once told me that he wouldn't send his children to church because his pastor conveyed a loser's mentality. He said: "Our pastor has a negative spirit. I don't want my children to be exposed to an ambitionless man." That attorney's impression of a loser's mentality may have been the pastor's desire to emulate a style of self-denial. Perhaps the pastor was attempting to model his life after the example of Christ's humility—not seeking equality with God, but instead emptying himself in the form of a servant (Phil. 2:5–11). Any model of self-denial, however, will be viewed with mixed emotions in our success-oriented culture and could make some clergy appear as losers. A self-denying style of ministry can be threatening to the laity when they perceive that their own value system is being rejected.

Do you know why John the Baptist is the saintly hero of the Eastern Orthodox believer? His icon appears in each of their churches. John the Baptist placed limits on his own ambition; he stepped aside for the ministry of Jesus. "He must increase, but I must decrease" (John 3:30). Such humility provides the Orthodox believer with inspiration and a reminder that there might well be limits to our personal ambition when we dare to submit to the Lordship of the Eternal Contemporary.

The final chapter discusses how renewal can be furthered by reshaping the pastoral task.

6
Reshaping the Pastoral Task

This is an exciting time to be a pastor. Admittedly, the ministry is experiencing a period of turbulence, with much speculation on its value. The ordained clergy are questioning, as never before, their identity and the meaning of vocation. Laity are also probing with the clergy during this period of restlessness and painful transition.

Toward a More Encompassing Model of Ministry

Contrary to biblical teachings, the corporation executive in far too many instances has become the model for the ministry. Clergy in gray flannel have given up the strenuous task of being pastor-theologians. Of course organizational administration is important, but is that the primary task of an ordained minister? Theological education is an expensive detour if administration is one's major preoccupation. Unfortunately, many ministers would be lost in the parish without the task of administrative chores; they would not want to relinquish them. Pastors have neglected their task as the grass-roots theologians within the community.

In fact, the "happy pastor" appears to be involved in some remodeling or building program where administration and its related activities consume almost the entire time. During the building process, the minister is able to bury lingering guilt feelings toward theological responsibilities. Some pastors even consider involvement with theology too risky an affair, especially during a building program. Theology divides, doesn't it? Thus theology is quickly dismissed as being divisive, a noncontributive factor to the "life, unity and purity" of the congregation. In many of today's parishes, "the relevant question is not so much the nature and character of the Christian faith, but how the church may become a community of 'accepting people' who gather to affirm each other."[1] The heresy of the contemporary church and its ministry lies in an excessive preoccupation with busyness, public relations, and "I'm okay, you're okay" sessions without theological direction.[2] Isn't this an effective route to hastening the church's death?

Look at our society. Who is it that makes significant and prophetic statements upon the global events of our times? Astronauts, artists, novelists, newscasters, but, for the most part, certainly not the clergy. Pastors have undermined their vital role as opinion makers in society. Harried, tired, and ill-prepared, they have become an inarticulate voice in a world seeking purpose and hope. Where are the pastor-theologians, the interpreters of the Word of God within the events of human life? Where is the theological leadership so desperately needed in the life of the church and society today? Without grass-roots theologians, what future will the churches have?

It is actually incumbent upon every grass-roots pastor to spell out "the gospel according to Jesus Christ" locally and globally. Unless this is done, pastors will find themselves addicted to secondary and introductory textbooks in psychology, sociology, and economics as their working frame of reference. Having once abrogated responsibility as grass-roots theologians, pastors then suffer from an identity crisis. The Eternal Contemporary no longer has a clear voice in the community. The pastor-theologians, on the other hand, who understand their task and learn to think theologically and concretely in the light of new events and happenings, will find deep satisfaction from their labors.

Without such theologizing, the church will always be attuned to the culture of the preceding age—always trying to catch up, but seldom providing leadership. Busy pastors have little time to reflect and to theologize. As a result, they tend to be overworked but underemployed, wondering at times if they are making any contribution to society. Even so, most pastors continue to insist that they are not theologians! Instead, they will strive diligently to program their way out of this dilemma rather than resort to serious thinking and theologizing within the core of their ministry. The minister is a surgeon with words; the scalpel can cut either to heal or to further endanger the patient. A pastor whose scalpel is either dull or rusty is guilty of theological malpractice. To overcome this danger is a concern of this book.

The discussion in these pages seeks to point us beyond our present styles of ministry, unfolding in the process a neglected model of ministry—*the pastor as the grass-roots theologian.* This model needs to be asserted in the church's present state of transition. In fact, this model provides the basic frame of reference within which all the models of ministry discussed in the previous chapters should be placed. Any model of ministry that does not operate from a sound theological and biblical premise needs to be questioned. This study serves as a corrective challenge to pastors and seminarians to emphasize their rightful role as the grass-roots interpreters, whose responsibility is to remind us individually and collectively of our divine vocation to be stewards and celebrants of God's creation.

To be sure, the many models of ministry in practice have their merits. Unfortunately, most of these models, in practice, have slighted the pastor as the grass-roots theologian; this factor may be suicidal for the church and the clergy. This may be construed as an overstatement; nevertheless, I believe that the current loss of confidence in our churches is due to this absence of effective theologizing and thinking among the practicing clergy. If the office of pastor is to make a significant contribution to our culture, the model of the pastor as the grass-roots theologian needs to be emphasized before the laity. I strongly suspect that the laity has a longing for Christian nurture, along with comfort and challenge.

A Marketplace Without Direction

As I question, listen, and probe the laity through my travels and teaching opportunities, a host of impressions have come clearly to the surface. The "Calian survey" makes no special claim, but I wonder if your own experience and observation bear out also what I have seen and heard. First, I have found that the laity and the clergy share a great deal of similarity in their common concerns and needs in life. This may be stating the obvious, but it is nevertheless important for us all to be aware that we are standing on a common platform. This fact is often forgotten during worship, when the pastor stands above the congregation. The posture sometimes suggests two classes of Christians and two classes of expectations. The fact is that we are one people under God, whose concerns and needs are remarkably and understandably similar. This factor is discovered in surprisingly fresh ways each day, leaving us startled and even shocked at times.

Take, for instance, the testimony of Robert K. Hudnut, a Presbyterian pastor who left his parish ministry for two years. He remarks in retrospect:

I have just had a harrowing experience. I have spent the last two years as a layperson.

This means I have lived with, among other things, the constant fear of losing my job, with a 40 percent salary cut, with no raises to offset inflation, with sixty-to-seventy-hour weeks, and with virtually no time, because of the demands of my job, for church.

You learn something.

What I have learned is that it isn't easy to be a layperson. A layperson has every bit as tough a row to hoe as a pastor. In many respects, a tougher one. The manse is gone. The pension is gone. The utility allowance is gone. Car allowance gone. Four weeks vacation and two weeks study leave—all gone.

Now I realize many pastors work a six-day week and many laypeople work only five. Hence their total vacation time may be even less. I also realize that many laypeople with comparable positions earn far more than pastors, even with their allowances. So, I am not generalizing, I am simply talking about me.

I not only lost financial security, I also lost some emotional security as well. No longer are you told on the first day of the week what a great job you're doing. No longer do you spend a great deal of your time "helping people." Your fellow employees are fine people and good friends, but you are not as close to them as you were to your brothers and sisters in church.

Furthermore, you have very little time for church itself. You are working long hours. Meetings conflict with church meetings. It is impossible to make a regular commitment of time. And when Sunday rolls around you are often so exhausted you just plain don't have the energy—even if you do have the will—to get up and get into the same clothes you wear to work and go to church. Besides, the churches you go to when you do get up are, let's face it, just not exciting.

Now all this is highly educational—particularly if you are someone like me who has been laying some pretty heavy demands on laypeople in such presumptuous books as *The Sleeping Giant* and *Arousing the Sleeping Giant.*[3]

Hudnut, like many pastors, has found that the marketplace isn't the easiest of worlds. Pastors should gain a new appreciation for the daily struggles of their laypeople, but they find themselves in unending restlessness, just like most persons in the marketplace. Have you noticed this? All of us shove and jockey into position so as not to miss anything in the ongoing race of humanity, only to reach a goal that may appear questionable in retrospect. Both clergy and laity are hungry for transcendence; the latest fad never seems to be the answer. Everyone is looking for a God who has cool water to offer, to satisfy our insatiable thirst in our endless race to nowhere. Everyone is looking for a paradise and never sure of its whereabouts—calling it, at first, a new parish, a promotion at work, or the establishment of a new friendship. The truth is that the endless search continues for *the source* of happiness. The people of God, clergy and laity, are called to minister to this human situation, to this endless pursuit.

In addition to this hunger for transcendence, there is a hunger for fellowship in the marketplace. Listen to the picture drawn by a former Catholic priest who immersed himself in the marketplace. This is what he wrote to me in a letter:

This is my first exposure to the hectic and demanding life of the aggressive young businessman. While I do enjoy the work, I don't think I can ever share their world view. It is not completely true to say that they are merely profit-oriented, but rather I think that they are oriented to successful achievement but in a manner which is unlike the manner in which a professional man would seek achievement. All of the metaphors at work are based on combat and fighting and are quite warlike in nature. The fellows tend to see the world as something to be fought and subdued each day. There is no chance to let up. Theirs is the world view of former ages in which the world was constantly attacking the basis of man's survival. Floods, plagues, drought, famine, etc., were the enemies. A farmer had to spend his whole day and his whole life providing for his family and preparing for the unknown, the hostile. It made sense for him to spend 20 hours in fields away from his wife and family. So, too, with my business friends, they perceive economic pitfalls to be everywhere—and they feel that many more are present but unseen. Disaster can strike from the least expected quarter and ruin the whole achievement. Every day is spent carefully—fighting and drilling to prevent disaster by constant awareness and readiness. The long hours put in by the fellows at work (a 60–70 hour week is normal) are seen both as a sign of dedication and as absolute necessity lest they become lax, smug, lazy or bureaucratic and become swept under by the vagaries of everyday business life. Like a pride of wild animals a great deal of time is spent testing one another and a great amount of stress and anxiety is engendered to keep all on their toes. To build successfully in this treacherous sand requires constant attention to details. Their joy and reward is to make money and to build a great business. The forces are many against them and a great deal of satisfaction comes from the fight to make a good deal, to make a good deal out of a bad one and to rally from a mistake or a serious loss.[4]

It is indeed a struggling, competitive world in which we find ourselves; friendship and fellowship are scarce commodities. There is a good deal of superficiality in our socializing process. Some have given up on ever finding meaningful camaraderie in our kind of world. One of the primary goals of the church as the people of God is to provide an authentic experience in human relationships. Unfortunately, many find the church no different from the "welcome wagon" in a community—the contacts are often fleeting and the commitments to each other minimal. This has often been depicted as the hypocritical nature of the church. The marketplace is truly hungry for caring relationships, and the challenge to the church is whether it will be part of the answer or part of the problem in the situation. The people of God can only meet this marketplace need when they themselves have a sense of direction and dedication to share.

The atmosphere of hostility and combat in the marketplace is due to the fact that we have not found ourselves —we are individuals in search of our identity and selfhood. An encounter of two persons can be described as two question marks greeting each other while searching for a place to rest anxieties and find acceptance within themselves and with each other. Are the people of God equal to this task? Or has it been our experience to leave a worship service in a greater state of quandary than when we entered? This hunger to find selfhood is a third major need in today's marketplace, along with the needs for transcendence and fellowship. The people of God must have a clear grasp of their own identity, or else they will not provide meaningful leadership in the future. It is a short step for any of us to surrender to the faceless forces of our present existence. What sound from the church will demand the attention of the marketplace?

Pastors and their people are mounting a cry to "do something!" But what? Some have urged the church to be "relevant," others have pressed for "renewal," and still others for "revival" and "reform." Relevance, renewal, revival, and reform have been bantered about in numerous sermons, debates, conferences, and official reports; their impact hardly causes a stir among us. We have immunized and insulated ourselves from our own ecclesiastical terminology. Some are suspicious or afraid of any sudden spiritual awakening or uncontrolled presence of the Spirit in our midst. Even charismatics have regularized their expectations of the Spirit! One pastor, a veteran of ten years in the parish, reported to me that "what has been lacking in much of this ferment to 'do something' has been any critical thinking. . . . There is a 'try something' mentality within some of our ranks which is reflected in all the areas of the church's life (liturgy, mission, evangelism, preaching, structure, education, etc.). This desire to see something happen has sent many clergy spinning out in all directions to find a model for their work which will produce the desired results. (There is often no clear ideal of what the 'results' might be. One is reminded of George Santayana's reported remark that a fanatic is a person who has lost sight of his goal and redoubled his effort to get there.)"⁵

Yet the pursuit of relevance, renewal, revival, and reform continues to dominate our thoughts and planning as we try to program our way out of our doldrums to meet the needs of a marketplace without direction. Some pastors have found creative and ingenuous ways to build bridges to the contemporary culture.

For example, there is the Rev. Al Carmines, of the Judson Memorial Church in New York City. Through the use of drama and musicals, he has been able to touch upon many contemporary issues of our society too explosive to handle in most parishes. His musical show, *The Faggot*, dealt with the subject of homosexuality. There is also Father Thomas Higgins, a Jesuit priest, who seeks to be relevant and relate to people, in the summer months, as a blackjack dealer in Las Vegas. The other nine months of the year he is an assistant chaplain and professor at Loyola Marymount University in Los Angeles. Another pastor on a summer circuit is the Rev. David Harris, who leads *The Circus Kingdom*, a troupe of thirty-six college-age students that tours the country, presenting both public and charity performances. The circus has no wild animals, but it does have clowns, aerialists, tumblers, fire-eaters, wire acts, jugglers, and a ten-piece band. The remainder of the year he serves as associate pastor of Capitol Hill Methodist Church in Washington, D.C. There is a German pastor, Dr. Reinhard Zorn in Wickrath, who is rather well known for producing and selling the best *Würste* (hot dogs, German style) in the area and regularly preaches on Sunday. In Virginia there is the well-known talk show on television under the direction of the Rev. M. C. Robertson, an ordained Baptist minister. Most people call him Pat, and his show, *700 Club,* experiences a mix of interviews, music, intense prayer, and reports of miracles. Some of his admirers refer to it as a religious *Tonight* show.

There are many more examples of pastors who have taken up secular employment along with their pastoral duties in order to relate more closely with their people. Others have gone into environmental firms and tree farming in their concern for our natural resources. Are all these efforts at "relevant ministry" helping the confused marketplace to find direction? Are these relevant efforts at ministry the key to renewal, revival, and reform in the church? Are the examples cited guidelines for future pastors? If not, how will the hunger of the marketplace be met? We need to look beyond for a model that is both more applicable to pastors and more useful to the rank and file of the laity. My answer is the pastor as the grass-roots theologian.

Only as we grasp the full potential of this concept of the pastor as a grass-roots theologian can the church be rescued from a greater state of disappointment and depression in this specialized world. Obviously, this is a grandiose claim for the Christian ministry; nevertheless, this claim must be recognized and seriously treated in the current discussions on the ministry.

The model of *pastor-theologian* seeks to eliminate the increasing polarization of the body of Christ into terms of laicism and clericalism. To overcome this polarization we must rediscover the content of clerical ordination within the biblical sacrament of baptism, and thereby reassert a sound and biblical view of the ministry as expressed in the concept of *laos*—the people of God. We must reassert the oneness of the body of Christ, which has been for too long functionally divided into a church of the laity and a church of the clergy.

Furthermore, we must cease to limit the title of theologian to professors in theological schools. The title "theologian" should apply to the entire people of God, and in particular to local pastors who live among the people of God. If we accept the implications of baptism and the priesthood of all believers, then the task of theologizing in its broadest dimensions belongs to all Christians. A grassroots theologian, in the inclusive sense, is any professing Christian who finds himself *relating* formally or informally, in his profession or avocation, in word or deed, the Christian message to the human situation. The responsibility of relating the gospel to the world is directed to all Christians who, through their baptism, have been inducted into the ministry of Jesus Christ. Baptism clearly sets forth our primary calling as followers of Christ. The local pastor with additional training is a professional grass-roots theologian, while the laity, in their amateur status, are also equally essential to the theologizing process within the body of Christ. Together in partnership, clergy and laity represent the household of faith. The theologian who teaches in the seminary or university is neither higher nor lower than the theologian in the parish. Together they perform a vital function in relating the Word to the world.

To picture the local pastor as the grass-roots theologian is to declare that the numerous other roles and styles of ministry must be subordinated and in some cases eliminated. Today's pastor must become more than the poor man's psychiatrist or the inept maintenance man, and his or her theology must extend beyond the mimeograph machine. The influence of pastors must go beyond the strength of their smile; too many ministers trade on their personalities rather than on their competence. To become a competent pastor-theologian, theological education must equip the pastor to think theologically on a lifetime basis. To be a student of any "systematic" view of theology is to be almost dated upon graduation. Similar to the emphasis of medical and law schools to think medically and legally, the seminaries and schools of theology must aim to prepare their students to think theologically. Professional education is more than the memorization of content; *it is the acquisition of a methodology in thinking.* A disciplined theological way of thinking can make a vital contribution to the complex human situation; it can make theology an exciting enterprise.

Such an emphasis upon theology may surprise some ministers today who are crying out for less theology and more psychology, sociology, and business administration as the vital "how to" subjects for pastors. Theology has been reduced to an afterthought for many pastors today. The accent must be upon a recovery of the authentic role of the pastor as the grass-roots theologian within the community. For too long the pastor has prostituted the position and confused it with other vocations. As grass-roots theologians, pastors have a purpose to fulfill among the people of God; they must function creatively although hampered by an increasingly structured institution that threatens to immobilize the Holy Spirit. The grass-roots theologian is more than a "company man," he or she is the catalyst of the Spirit in that locality.

Grass-Roots Theologians: Messengers of Identity

The pastor works through a theological medium. This is an inescapable fact of the profession. In whatever way ministry is defined, its theological dimension is paramount. The clergy are God's theological witnesses on earth. The pastor, whether as a surrogate of God or as a servant of God, is first and foremost God's witness to the transcendent dimension of reality. Theology is the articulation of this reality in whatever shape or form it takes. For example, counting the Sunday collection in the church office after the service is a theological as well as a financial task in the life of the church. The pastor as the resident theologian must make that relationship clear for the people in the parish. Consider also the matter of organization in the parish; carrying this out is as much a theological task as an administrative skill. The pastor as the resident theologian must not limit theologizing to preaching and teaching. Unfortunately, some books on ministry imply this. The pastor as the grass-roots theologian must have a theological rationale for all phases of ministry. To fail to do so is to undermine the pastoral office, and to turn the church into just another business, another organization completely void of its raison d'être.

The church divorced of its theological roots and understanding has lost its uniqueness and its identity. The overriding task of every pastor is to be the church's grass-roots theologian, who constantly guides the people of God in understanding their identity. Without identity, the church will be sucked into the uncertainty and relativism of our society. Without identity, the church will lose its mission and vision for tomorrow. The grass-roots theologian is the messenger of identity for the local parish. The resident theologian functions as an instrument of the Spirit to remind the church of its past and its future destiny under God. Whatever other label pastors may wish to attach to themselves, whatever other skills they wish to acquire, the unifying umbrella of the pastoral office is theological in nature.

In short, every pastor is a theologian. The other skills acquired in seminary and elsewhere are subordinate to this primary image—to be God's theological witnesses on earth. Pastors serve as theological witnesses in their various specialities: counseling, education, and so forth. Whatever the speciality of any pastor, it should be seen as reinforcing the pastor's primary role as the grass-roots theologian. To be a pastor is to function within a theological frame of reference; keen awareness of this fact will clarify a great deal of ambiguity surrounding the profession. Any definition of ministry must be cognizant of this theological framework.

To put it quite simply, theology is the task one chooses upon entering the professional ministry. A pastor can go through an entire lifetime of ministry and miss playing the game of one's life! The pastor as the grass-roots theologian will not miss *the* game. Theologizing is the means by which one's servanthood can make a significant contribution to the larger community and gain by God's grace some measure of greatness. Greatness begins when the pastor as the messenger of identity questions (from the servant position of powerlessness) the establishment of that society as God's theological witness in that community. Erik Erikson, the psychoanalyst of identity, has put it well: "And the greatest, more often than not, are those rare persons who have questioned the status quo and have become immortal by creating a new one."[6] The pastor as the grass-roots theologian, whose attention and energies seek to clarify Christian convictions in an age of uncertainty, individualism, and relativism, is questioning the status quo and thereby able to create a new frame of reference from the texts of Scripture.

Is this the kind of ministry the laity should expect their pastors to practice in the future?

The tragedy today is that many pastors are reluctant theologians in the practice of their ministry. Seward Hiltner puts forth the results of a probable poll of ministers of all denominations who were asked the question, "Do you regard yourself as a theologian?" The results, he suggests, would probably emerge as follows:

31% said, "Well, I am a minister, but you could hardly call me a theologian."

22% said, "It is true I have studied theology, but I'm not really a theologian."

17% replied, "Brother, I sure ain't. I'm only a simple parson, not one of those high-powered book guys."

8% admitted, "Well, I guess I am, in a way, but I am more interested in serving people than in theology."

7% said, "Where did you get that idea? And don't do it again. I'd even rather be called 'Reverend' than 'theologian.'"

5% said, "No."

4% replied, "I am about twice a year, when I go back for the alumni lectures."

2% said, "Pardon me, I have to rush to a funeral."

1% snorted, "I wonder who thought up that question?"[7]

Part of the reluctance of the pastor to be a theologian is based on the anti-intellectual aspects of American culture, which tend to encourage activism. Contemplation, study, and reflection are not obvious or visible on the daily agenda. They are the areas in which pastors cheat, in order to accomplish the other demands of each day. This activist tendency also afflicts our theological schools and faculties and in part explains why the era of greatness among academic theologians seems to have passed. How, then, can we expect greatness from parish pastors when the theological suppliers (the seminaries) are lacking in greatness as well? The question asked by that active layman at the beginning of our study haunts me as a professor in the seminary. To what extent am I reinforcing the image of the ministry as a profession of "accredited mediocrity"? My colleagues and I must reexamine ourselves without being masochistic. We need to raise the standards of commitment and excellence of seminarians; we must not accept fervor as a substitute for competence.

To theologize at the core of one's ministry is to underline the unique role of the pastor in a community and among professionals. "What is it that you do?" asks the doctor, lawyer, educator, accountant, business executive, etc. Pastors should reply that they are the professional theologians of the community—the trained messengers of identity in a society suffering from collective amnesia. People want to know who they are. This quest is expressed in many different ways. The pastor as the messenger of identity must supply the bridge on which a meaningful dialogue can take place. The pastor's basic call in the community is to be the grass-roots theologian who can help persons in their quest for identity. That identity must ultimately be placed within a theological context. This is the pastor's ministry in a society becoming increasingly more anxious about its identity.[8] How effective pastors are in communicating their task depends upon doing their theological homework—reading, reflection, contemplation, and listening.

Henri J. M. Nouwen, in his book *The Wounded Healer*, emphasizes the importance of this theological homework when he refers to tomorrow's spiritual leader as the articulator of inner events, a compassionate person who is also a contemplative critic. His emphasis upon articulation is crucial if the pastor wishes to be the grass-roots theologian of the community. According to him:

The man who can articulate the movements of his inner life, *who can give names* [italics added] to his varied experiences, need no longer be a victim of himself, but is able slowly and consistently to remove the obstacles that prevent the spirit from entering. He is able to create space for Him whose heart is greater than his, whose eyes see more than his, and whose hands can heal more than his.

This articulation, I believe, is the basis for a spiritual leadership of the future, because only he who is able to articulate his own experience can offer himself to others as a source of clarification. The Christian leader is, therefore, first of all, a man who is willing to put his own articulated faith at the disposal of those who ask his help. In this sense he is a servant of servants, because he is the first to enter the promised but dangerous land, the first to tell those who are afraid what he has seen, heard and touched.[9]

For the pastor to be a grass-roots theologian of Nouwen's caliber a major reassessment and reordering of present priorities and daily schedules in ministry is needed. If identity is the pivotal issue in our society, irrespective of what a person's economic or social stratum is, then the pastor needs clear insights into the inner self, to be a catalyst of the Spirit for others.

Yet the need for economic security and financial solvency for our churches and related institutions has preoccupied the contemporary scene. We have been too myopic in the name of financial exigencies and have traded off our vision for the perspective of meeting the demands of the bottom line. Commonsense realism has subverted our Christian hope that God is the ultimate supplier of all our material needs and that the cross is the ultimate negation of common sense. In the process of this trade-off (common sense versus the cross), we have diluted our mission and lost our identity. We, like our society, are suffering from the collective amnesia of where we have come from and where we are aimed. We are waiting for our pastors to herald a clear note and to put to one side the cautious attitudes dictated by common sense. We need to become bold witnesses to the living God. The laity, in the depths of their own restlessness, expect it of us. Let us fulfill our rightful role as the messengers of identity, the grass-roots theologians of our community.

More specifically, the grass-roots theologian is expected to maintain the truth and integrity of the gospel, whatever the cost. James D. Smart, a distinguished churchman and author, has clearly stated, "The church's first business is with the truth, not with machinery, even the most sanctified ecclesiastical machinery."[10] Today's church politics is unhealthy. Theological reflection in the church has often become a derivative of pragmatic considerations. Common sense has been and always will be at the peril of the gospel. Common sense is often a demonic ideology that has led large segments of the church's clergy and laity astray. It has replaced theology, making it at best an afterthought in the church's decision-making process. As one pastor admitted in candor: "I think essentially I am a humanist with Christ on my lips. I don't have a theological focus at all. If I did, I am afraid it might get in the way of what I am doing. My theology, if you want to call it that, is to share my life with people in need."[11] This is certainly a noble goal, shared by countless other institutions. It is certainly not an adequate rationale for pastors or churches in distinguishing their uniqueness within the community. In fact, a strong case could be made that many other organizations and institutions are meeting human needs (at least the material aspects) more adequately than either the pastor or the church, without a lot of religious trimmings.

The pastor who does not accept and acknowledge that theology is the medium of one's profession, as medicine is for the physician or law for the attorney, is committing professional suicide. On the other hand, the pastor who takes the theological framework seriously will be engaged in a ministry that is wider in scope than a medical or legal framework and equally as demanding. Pastors who acknowledge theologizing as the core of their ministry realize that they stand between two mysteries—the mystery of God and the mystery of humankind. As the messenger of identity in quest of insight and meaning, the pastor will always be confronted by these walls of mystery. Pastors as resident theologians must always live in the tension between mystery and meaning. To reduce the tension is to distort what we know and to press beyond our human limitations.

"To be a theologian," according to James D. Smart, "is simply to take the question of Christian truth with complete seriousness, acknowledging that we are responsible to God not only for sins in our conduct but also for untruth in our doctrine. We cannot withhold the seemingly harsh judgment, then, that a minister who does not in any way do the work of a theologian is a minister who does not take seriously the problem of error in his own gospel and in the life of the church."[12] The pastor who is a theologian *first* (before being a counselor, educator, manager, evangelist, etc.) knows the short distance one has penetrated into mysteries, which in turn enables the pastor to avoid glibness or dogmatism in speaking. The function of theological education is primarily to open our eyes to the magnitude of the mysteries that we are commissioned to probe and to proclaim. The grass-roots theologian must be content with the words that he or she can speak with honesty— words from God to us and words on our behalf to God.

Pastors must avoid the twin faults of giving definitive answers on insignificant questions or dogmatic answers on complex issues, which reduce the tension between mystery and meaning. With every reduction of tension, there is usually a distortion of truth. With increased knowledge today, we have also increased our ignorance. There is no need to be apologetic when we find it necessary to say, "I don't know." The experts in every field know and acknowledge the limitations of their knowledge. This need not decrease our desire to add to our store of information, for learning is an important part of being human. Society has greatly increased its store of information; however, understanding is lagging considerably. The grass-roots theologian, the messenger of identity, is in a pivotal position to call this factor to our attention. To put forth a ray of understanding may prove helpful to a society in search of its roots and identity. A theologizing ministry of this caliber will save the church from trivialization and decline. It will enable the church to lead society in recovering its destiny and its hopes for a more meaningful tomorrow.

Pastors must aid individuals in discovering their names again. We live in a functionally oriented society, in which names have been subordinated to functions. This is one reason that makes retirement so difficult for individuals. People spend a great span of their lives performing a function—as teacher, carpenter, assembly-line worker, lawyer, executive, etc. We are known through our functions, which normally cease at the time of retirement. Who are we then—when retirement comes? The grass-roots theologian as the messenger of identity has a ministry to perform. The gospel message affirms who we are, above and beyond our function. The pastor's theological task, whatever his or her speciality, is to interpret to each individual in a state of quandary that God knows that person's name. The gospel says, "God sees you, understands you, and accepts you." Herein lies the core message of identity—we are the children of God, we are wanted and loved. We have entered into a son/daughter relationship before God. We need no longer languish in a state of amnesia; we need no longer be anxious about our past or our future.

The messenger of identity proclaims clearly in words and ways that our sense of lostness has been overcome through God's grace, revealed and celebrated by us in Jesus the Christ. The gospel's message of identity ties together past, present, and future; it is a timeless and powerful message. Relating this message effectively is the challenge that faces today's pastor and holds the answer to the question, "Can the public expect greatness?"

Postscript

It was a pleasant Sunday afternoon. I was visiting with a husband and wife who were committed and active in church life. In fact, they were involved as officers in various committees and groups of the church. Their children had established their own homes and careers, with the exception of their youngest son, Bob, who was attending college.

Bob found church meaningful and respected his pastors. In fact, Bob sometimes considered becoming a pastor. I felt that he could make an outstanding contribution in ministry. Blessed with a good mind, he was compassionate, attractive, and imaginative. I felt that Bob could *also* become a good medical doctor, physicist, or biologist. He was capable in the areas of science and mathematics as well as literature and history. On the weekend of our visit, Bob was still at school, in the midst of semester exams.

In our conversation, Bob's parents mentioned that he was still in a quandary about choosing a particular career. "How about the ministry?" I inquired. "Bob would make a great pastor!" There was a long pause. Bob's father began to explain that entering the ministry is really a private affair between God and the individual. The parents felt that they shouldn't interfere.

Our conversation continued for a while. Then I inquired, "What if Bob were thinking of becoming a medical

doctor or a physicist, how would you feel?" Bob's mother
replied: "Why, we would be thrilled and encourage him.
We know that Bob has the ability. Those professions are
certainly worthy of pursuit. In fact, we believe he would
be dedicated in either field."

I appreciated their candor. "Why is it," I said, "that as
parents you would encourage him to become a doctor or
a physicist, but won't interfere in a possible decision for
the pastoral ministry? Certainly, becoming a pastor is neither a higher nor a lower calling of service than being a
doctor or a physicist. Belief in the priesthood of *all* believers implies our universal obligation as followers to commit
ourselves to God's service whatever our choice of career
goals. The call to pastoral ministry is no more a 'private
affair' than the call to any other field of worthy endeavor."

Parents are never neutral when it comes to the career
goals of their children. Every parent wishes the utmost
well-being for a son or daughter. In fact, parents sometimes become too involved in interpreting what their children's welfare ought to be. Bob's parents were in agreement with this observation.

"Quite frankly," they said, "we have been active at
church and have seen both the joys and the frustrations of
our pastors. We really wonder if, in the balance, it is really
worth it. Don't misunderstand us; we love the church, but
the hassles our pastors have to face at times are unbeliev-
able! We would like to save our own flesh and blood from
that kind of grief. Our Bob can serve the church as a
devoted layperson, as we have."

Later that evening, I reflected on the afternoon conversation. The following impression began to formulate
within my thinking: namely, that the laity who are most
active in the church are often the very persons who prefer
that their own sons and daughters avoid careers in the
church. The reasons for this trend are many. Recent years
have revealed the church's inner workings; this public

exposure has taken its toll, and the ministerial mystiq
no longer there. The most active among the laity, as a
consequence, have reacted quietly in steering their children from careers in the church. What hope is there, then,
for outstanding leadership and commitment in the future
if this apparent trend continues? Can the laity expect
greatness from the clergy? The penultimate answer lies as
much with today's laity as it does with tomorrow's clergy.
God's call addresses laity and clergy to the responsibility
and fulfillment of working together in ministry.

Notes

1. The Situation Today

1. David S. Schuller, Milo L. Brekke, and Merton P. Strommen, eds., *Readiness for Ministry*, Vol. 1, *Criteria* (The Association of Theological Schools in the United States and Canada), pp. 6–20.

2. *1976 General Assembly Blue Book*, Pt. 2 (The United Presbyterian Church U.S.A., Office of the General Assembly), pp. 106–130.

3. Ibid., p. 106.

4. Ibid., p. 115.

5. Vincent A. Yzermans, "On Leaving a Parish," *The New York Times*, May 23, 1976.

6. William R. Garrett, "Politicized Clergy: A Sociological Interpretation of the 'New Breed,' " *Journal for the Scientific Study of Religion*, Vol. 12, No. 4 (Dec. 1973), pp. 383–399.

7. Information on Rev. Robert S. Lutz is taken from Dennis E. Shoemaker's report on the state of the church and its clergy, entitled "In Quest of Ministry: Pastors Today," *A.D.*, Jan. 1975, p. 42.

8. For a fuller discussion of Socratic evangelism, see my book *Grace, Guts and Goods: How to Stay Christian in an Affluent Society* (Thomas Nelson, 1971), pp. 63–65.

9. *Christianity Today*, March 28, 1969, p. 592.

10. For a fuller discussion of our business culture, see my book *The Gospel According to The Wall Street Journal* (John Knox Press, 1975).

11. Wilfred Bockelman, "The Pros and Cons of Robert Schuller," *The Christian Century*, Aug. 20–27, 1975, pp. 732–735.

12. Stuart Weiss, "Reverend Ike: Them That's Got Are Them That Gets," *Wharton Account,* Oct. 1975.

13. An example of the tension is expressed by Larry La Velle, a Methodist pastor, in his article "The Question of 'Success' in the Ministry," *The Christian Ministry,* March 1972.

14. An interview with "Peter Drucker on Church Management," *The Christian Ministry,* Sept. 1972, pp. 5–12. See also Drucker's book *Management: Tasks, Responsibilities, Practices* (Harper & Row, 1974).

15. Ibid.

16. Leander E. Keck, quoted in *Monday Morning,* May 3, 1976.

2. The Tough Side of Ministry

1. *The Wall Street Journal,* Oct. 3, 1974.

2. *Telegraph-Herald, AP,* Jan. 28, 1975.

3. Quoted by David M. Skoloda, *The Milwaukee Journal,* Oct. 13, 1974, p. 3.

4. Quoted by Paul G. Hayer, *The Milwaukee Journal,* April 14, 1974, p. 1.

5. Ibid.

6. Part of a cover story in *Time,* Dec. 29, 1975, pp. 47–56, entitled "Saints Among Us." See also Desmond Doig, *Mother Teresa* (Harper & Row, 1976).

7. An example of this new style of theologizing is found in my book *Grace, Guts and Goods.*

8. See Paul R. Lawrence and Jay W. Lorsch, "New Management Job: The Integrator," *Harvard Business Review,* Nov.–Dec. 1967, pp. 142–151.

9. The material in this section has been adapted from my article "How to Go Through Seminary Without Losing Your Faith," *The Christian Century,* Feb. 7, 1973. Used by permission.

10. Schubert Ogden, "What Is Theology?" *Journal of Religion,* Jan. 1972, pp. 22–40.

11. See *Theological Education,* Spring 1972; and *Presbyterian Outlook,* Oct. 23, 1972.

12. For further insights into Berdyaev's thoughts, see my work *Berdyaev's Philosophy of Hope* (Augsburg Publishing House, 1969).

13. See Martin E. Marty and Dean Peerman, eds., *New Theology, No. 4* (Macmillan Company, 1967); and Gordon D. Kaufman, *God the Problem* (Harvard University Press, 1972).

14. For a comparison of Eastern and Western approaches to theological foundations, see my work *Icon and Pulpit: The Protestant-Orthodox Encounter* (Westminster Press, 1968).

15. H. Richard Niebuhr, *The Meaning of Revelation* (Macmillan Company, 1941), p. 77.

3. Women and Men in Ministry

1. *Presbyterian Outlook*, Dec. 7, 1981, pp. 3–4.

2. Ibid.

3. Quoted in *The Philadelphia Inquirer*, Nov. 30, 1975.

4. Thomas Franklin O'Meara, "Feminine Ministry and Clerical Culture," *Commonweal*, Sept. 28, 1973.

5. Georges Barrois, "Women and the Priestly Office According to the Scriptures," *St. Vladimir's Theological Quarterly*, Vol. 19, Nov. 3, 1975, p. 192. In his own lifetime, Dr. Barrois has been a Catholic and a Protestant, and is presently a member of the Eastern Orthodox tradition.

6. Ibid.

7. *Los Angeles Times*, June 29, 1976, Pt. I, p. 7.

8. Shelby Rooks, "Up-Beat Ministry," *Theology Today*, April 1976.

9. Evidence in support of women pastors abounds. For biblical materials, see Krister Stendahl, *The Bible and the Role of Women* (Fortress Press, 1976); Robin Scroggs, "Paul and the Eschatological Women," *Journal of the American Academy of Religion*, 1972, pp. 283–303; Wayne A. Meeks, "The Image of the Androgyne: Some Uses of a Symbol in Earliest Christianity," *History of Religions*, Vol. 13 (1974), pp. 165–208; Robin Scroggs, "Paul and the Eschatological Woman: Revisited," pp. 532–537, and Elaine H. Pagels, "Paul and Women: A Response to Recent Discussions," *Journal of the American Academy of Religion*, 1974, pp. 538–549.

For theological, historical, and sociological considerations, see Hans Küng, "Feminism: A New Reformation," *The New York Times Magazine*, May 23, 1976, pp. 34–35; Sheila D. Collins, "Toward a Feminist Theology," *The Christian Century*, Aug. 2, 1972, pp. 796–799; Karen L. Bloomquist, "Women's Rising Consciousness: Implications for the Curriculum," *Theological Education*, Summer 1972, pp. 233–240; Marjorie Suchocki, "A Servant Office: The Ordination of Women," *Religion in Life*, 1978, pp. 192–210; two issues of *The Christian Ministry* are devoted to women and ministry, May 1971 and May 1975; and the joint statement by the Roman Catholic/Presbyterian-Reformed Consultation on Women in the Church, Oct. 30, 1971, Richmond, Virginia. In addition to articles, see the Selected Bibliography on Ministry for books.

10. For stories on couples in joint ministry, see Barbara Gerlach Mack and John Mack, "Equal in Marriage Equal in Ministry," *A.D.*, Nov. 1972; Gerry Nadel, "Mr. and Mrs. Minister," *The New York Times Magazine*, Feb. 1, 1976; and William Simbro, "Two Iowa Couples Ordained," *Des Moines Sunday Register*, June 20, 1976.

11. For further discussion on future trends in the family, see Joan Libman and Herbert G. Lawson, "The Family, Troubled by Changing Mores, Still Likely to Thrive," *The Wall Street Journal*, March 18, 1976; "The Superfamily—A New Life-Style? *The Futurist*, April 1976; Michael Novak, "The Family out of Favor," *Harper's*, April 1, 1976; and "The Family Today," *A.D.*, Vol.4, No. 5 (May 1975).

12. See the following stories in *The Wall Street Journal:* John Barnett, "Growing Job Demands Shatter the Marriages of More Executives," May 10, 1967; Robert Seidenber, M.D., "Dear Mr. Success: Consider Your Wife," Feb. 7, 1972; Mary Bralove, "For Executives' Wives, Firms' Transfers Are a Painful Way of Life," Aug. 1, 1973; and "For Married Couples, Two Careers Can Be Exercise in Frustration," May 13, 1975.

13. *Des Moines Sunday Register*, Sept. 24, 1967. © Ann Landers, Field Newspaper Syndicate. Used by permission.

14. *Wisconsin State Journal*, Nov. 19, 1967. © Ann Landers, Field Newspaper Syndicate. Used by permission. See the July 1971 issue of *The Christian Ministry*, which is devoted to "The Minister's Family," with informative articles on the minister's wife.

4. The Leadership of the Laity

1. For background, see Stephen Charles Neill and Hans-Ruedi Weber, eds., *The Layman in Christian History* (Westminster Press, 1963), especially the chapter on "The Ancient Church" by George Huntston Williams.

2. See Lewis S. Mudge, ed., *Model for Ministry: A Report for Study Issued by the General Assembly Special Committee on the Theology of the Call*, The United Presbyterian Church U.S.A., Office of the General Assembly, 1970.

3. Peter Hebblethwaite, "The Church of the Future," *Commonweal*, Dec. 19, 1975, p. 618.

4. Ibid.

5. William J. Bouwsma, "Christian Adulthood," *Daedalus*, Spring 1976, p. 83.

6. Ibid.

7. Ibid.

8. For an active layperson's challenging article, see J. Irwin Miller, "Should Churches 'Play It Safe'?" *Reader's Digest*, April 1972.

5. The Material Side of Ministry

1. James I. McCord, *Princeton Theological Seminary Alumni News*, Autumn 1974. Used by permission.

2. Harry G. Goodykoontz, *The Minister in the Reformed Tradition* (John Knox Press, 1963), pp. 100–101.

3. See Ernest Werner, "Remodeling the Protestant Ministry," *The American Scholar*, Winter 1964–65, pp. 35–36. See also Robert M. Healey, "The Ministerial Mystique," *The Christian Century*, Feb. 6, 1974.

4. See, for example, the "Report of Compensation Committee to 188th General Assembly (1975), The United Presbyterian Church U.S.A., Office of the General Assembly. Briefly, this report outlines the following principles for compensation: (1) Pay should be related to the "weight" or responsibilities and impact of the job and the performance of the job holder; (2) there should not be excessive differences between the highest and the lowest paid clergy jobs; (3) a moderate standard of living should be provided; (4) a vigorous program on behalf of women and minority persons in church employment should be included; (5) wealthier segments of the church should take a new degree of responsibility for supporting ministry in poorer or discriminated-against segments of society.

5. George E. Sweazey, "The Place of Ambition in the Ministry," *The Princeton Seminary Bulletin*, Feb. 1967, p. 36.

6. Ibid., pp. 37–40.

6. Reshaping the Pastoral Task

1. Dennis E. Shoemaker, "In Quest of Ministry: Pastors Today," *A.D.*, Jan. 1975, pp. 41–42.

2. Kenneth A. Briggs, "Growing Number in Clergy Using 'I'm

OK, You're OK' Counseling Concept," *The New York Times*, Feb. 29, 1976.

3. Robert K. Hudnut, "Where the Action Is," *Seminary Quarterly*, Spring 1976 (published by Ministers Life and Casualty Union), p. 1. Used by permission.

4. The author of this letter will remain anonymous.

5. These reflections are from a former graduate student of mine, Dr. James Bortell, First United Methodist Church, Mason City, Ill.

6. Erik Erikson, "Dr. Borg's Life Cycle," *Daedalus*, Spring 1976, p. 18.

7. Seward Hiltner, *Ferment in the Ministry* (Abingdon Press, 1969), p. 159.

8. For a study on identity, see William Glasser, M.D., *The Identity Society* (Harper & Row, 1972).

9. Henri J. M. Nouwen, *The Wounded Healer* (Doubleday & Co., 1972), p. 38.

10. James D. Smart, *The Rebirth of Ministry* (Westminster Press, 1960), p. 134.

11. Quoted in Dennis E. Shoemaker, "In Quest of Ministry: Pastors Today," *A.D.*, Jan. 1975, p. 45.

12. Smart, *The Rebirth of Ministry*, p. 135. See also J. Stanley Glen, *The Recovery of the Teaching Ministry* (Westminster Press, 1960); Harry G. Goodykoontz, *The Minister in the Reformed Tradition;* Robert S. Paul, *Ministry* (Wm. B. Eerdmans, 1965); James D. Smart, *The Teaching Ministry of the Church* (Westminster Press, 1964); and Robert W. Henderson, *The Teaching Office for the Reformed Tradition* (Westminster Press, 1962).

Selected Bibliography on Ministry

(This selected list does not include those works already cited in the notes.)

Ministry in Historical Perspective

Baxter, Richard. *The Reformed Pastor.* John Knox Press, 1956.

Calvin, John. *Calvin: Institutes of the Christian Religion.* The Library of Christian Classics, Vols. XX-XXI. Westminster Press, 1960.

Chrysostom, St. John. *The Priesthood.* Macmillan Co., 1955.

Clebsch, William A., and Jaekle, Charles R. *Pastoral Care in Historical Perspective.* Prentice-Hall, 1964.

Congar, Yves M. J. *Lay People in the Church.* Newman Press, 1957.

Gilkey, Langdon. *How the Church Can Minister to the World Without Losing Itself.* Harper & Row, 1964.

Goodykoontz, Harry J. *The Minister in the Reformed Tradition.* John Knox Press, 1963.

Henderson, Robert W. *The Teaching Office in the Reformed Tradition.* Westminster Press, 1962.

Holland, DeWitte, ed. *Preaching in American History.* Abingdon Press, 1969.

Jenkins, Daniel T. *The Gift of Ministry.* London: Faber & Faber, 1947.

————. *The Protestant Ministry.* London: Faber & Faber, 1958.

Johnson, Robert Clyde, ed. *The Church and Its Changing Ministry.* The United Presbyterian Church U.S.A., Office of the General Assembly, 1961.

Kraemer, Hendrik. *A Theology of the Laity.* Westminster Press, 1958.

155

Loetscher, Lefferts. *The Broadening Church.* University of Pennsylvania Press, 1957.

MacGregor, Geddes. *Corpus Christi.* Westminster Press, 1958.

Meer, Frederik van der. *Augustine the Bishop.* Sheed & Ward, 1961.

McNeill, John T. *A History of the Cure of Souls.* Harper & Row, Torchbooks, 1965.

Nelson, John Oliver, ed. *Work and Vocation.* Harper & Brothers, 1954.

Niebuhr, H. Richard. *The Purpose of the Church and Its Ministry.* Harper & Brothers, 1956.

Niebuhr, H. Richard, and William, Daniel Day, eds. *The Ministry in Historical Perspectives.* Harper & Brothers, 1956.

Paul, Robert S. *Ministry.* Wm. B. Eerdmans Publishing Co., 1965.

Schweizer, Eduard. *Church Order in the New Testament.* London: SCM Press, 1961.

Smith, Elwyn Allen. *The Presbyterian Ministry in American Culture (1700–1900).* Westminster Press, 1963.

Contemporary Ministry

Baker, Wesley. *Split-Level Fellowship.* Westminster Press, 1965.

Belgum, David. *The Church and Its Ministry.* Prentice-Hall, 1963.

Berger, Peter L. *The Noise of Solemn Assemblies.* Doubleday & Co., 1961.

Brown, Robert McAfee. *Frontiers for the Church Today.* Oxford University Press, 1973.

Come, Arnold B. *Agents of Reconciliation.* Westminster Press, 1960.

Dittes, James E. *Minister on the Spot.* Pilgrim Press, 1970.

Dulles, Avery. *Models of the Church.* Doubleday & Co., 1974.

Fichtner, Joseph H. *Priest and People.* Sheed & Ward, 1965.

Gibbs, Mark, and Morton, T. Ralph. *God's Frozen People.* Westminster Press, 1965.

————. *God's Lively People.* Westminster Press, 1971.

Glock, Charles Y.; Ringer, Benjamin; and Babbie, Earl R. *To Comfort and to Challenge.* University of California Press, 1967.

Holmes, Urban T. *The Future Shape of Ministry.* Seabury Press, 1971.

Illich, Ivan. *The Church, Change and Development.* Herder & Herder, 1970.

Jud, Gerald; Mills, Edgar, Jr.; and Burch, Genevieve. *Ex-Pastors.* United Church Press, 1970.

Leas, Speed, and Kittlaus, Paul. *Church Fights.* Westminster Press, 1973.

Mitchell, Kenneth R. *Psychological and Theological Relationships in the Multiple Staff Ministry.* Westminster Press, 1966.

Niebuhr, Reinhold. *Leaves from the Notebook of a Tamed Cynic.* Meridian Books, 1957.

Nouwen, Henri. *Creative Ministry.* Doubleday & Co., 1971.

Pope, Liston. *Millhands and Preachers: A Study of Gastonia.* Yale University Press, 1942.

Rahner, Karl. *Servants of the Lord.* Herder & Herder, 1968.

Rouch, Mark. *Competent Ministry.* Abingdon Press, 1974.

Schaller, Lyle. *The Pastor and the People.* Abingdon Press, 1973.

Shahovsky, John. *The Orthodox Pastor.* St. Vladimir's Seminary Press, 1966.

Sills, Horace S., ed. *Grassroots Ecumenicity.* United Church Press, 1967.

Sittler, Joseph. *The Ecology of Faith.* Fortress Press, 1961.

Thorman, Donald J. *The Emerging Layman: The Role of the Catholic Layman in America.* Doubleday & Co., 1962.

Welsh, Clement. *Preaching in a New Key.* Pilgrim Press, 1974.

Worley, Robert C. *Change in the Church: A Source of Hope.* Westminster Press, 1971.

———. *The Church for Others, Two Reports on the Missionary Structures of the Congregation.* Geneva: World Council of Churches, 1968.

———. *The Priestly Ministry, Report of the International Theological Commission.* Theological Publications in India, St. Peter's Seminary, 1971.

Women in Ministry

Daly, Mary. *Beyond God the Father.* Beacon Press, 1973.

Hageman, Alice L., ed. *Sexist Religion and Women in the Church.* Association Press, 1974.

Jewett, Paul K. *Man as Male and Female.* Wm. B. Eerdmans Publishing Co., 1975.

McLaughlin, Eleanor, and Ruether, Rosemary, eds. *Women of Spirit.* Simon & Schuster, 1979.

Rosenberg, F. R.; Sullivan, E. M., and Besanceney, P. H., eds.

Women and Ministry: A Survey of the Experience of Roman Catholic Women in the United States. Washington, D.C.: Center for Applied Research in the Apostolate (CARA), 1980.

Ruether, Rosemary Radford, ed. *Religion and Sexism.* Simon & Schuster, 1974.

Russell, Letty M. *Human Liberation in a Feminist Perspective—A Theology.* Westminster Press, 1974.

Stendahl, Krister. *The Bible and the Role of Women.* Fortress Press, 1966.

Ministry in Action and Reflection

Adams, James Luther, and Hiltner, Seward, eds. *Pastoral Care in the Liberal Churches.* Abingdon Press, 1970.

Allen, Roland. *Missionary Methods: St. Paul's or Ours.* Wm. B. Eerdmans Publishing Co., 1962.

Barth, Karl. *Preaching the Gospel.* Westminster Press, 1963.

Brooks, Phillips. *Lectures on Preaching.* Baker Book House, 1969.

Clinebell, Howard J. *Basic Types of Pastoral Counseling.* Abingdon Press, 1966.

Davis, Henry Grady. *Design for Preaching.* Fortress Press, 1958.

Dittes, James E. *The Church in the Way.* Charles Scribner's Sons, 1967.

Doberstein, John W., ed. *Minister's Prayer Book.* Fortress Press, 1959.

Forsyth, P. T. *Positive Preaching and the Modern Mind.* Alec R. Allenson, 1949.

Fukuyama, Yoshio. *The Ministry in Transition.* University of Pennsylvania Press, 1972.

Glasse, James D. *Profession: Minister.* Abingdon Press, 1968.

———. *Putting It Together in the Parish.* Abingdon Press, 1972.

Hoekendijk, J. C. *The Church Inside Out.* Westminster Press, 1964.

Hudnut, Robert K. *Surprised by God.* Association Press, 1972.

Hulme, William E. *Your Pastor's Problems.* Augsburg Publishing House, 1966.

Nelson, James B. *Moral Nexus: Ethics of Christian Identity and Community.* Westminster Press, 1971.

Oates, Wayne E. *The Christian Pastor,* Third Edition, Revised. Westminster Press, 1982.

Quinley, Harold E. *The Prophetic Clergy: Social Activism Among Protestant Ministers.* John Wiley & Sons, 1974.

Rahner, Karl. *The Spiritual Exercises.* Herder & Herder, 1965.
Raines, Robert A. *The Secular Congregation.* Harper & Row, 1968.
Sittler, Joseph. *The Anguish of Preaching.* Fortress, 1966.
Smith, Charles Merrill. *How to Become a Bishop Without Being Religious.* Doubleday & Co., 1965.
Smith, Donald P. *Clergy in the Cross Fire.* Westminster Press, 1973.
Williams, Daniel Day. *The Minister and the Care of Souls.* Harper & Brothers, 1961.
Wolf, Carl J. C. *Jonathan Edwards on Evangelism.* Wm. B. Eerdmans Publishing Co., 1958.
Wynn, John Charles. *Pastoral Ministry to Families.* Westminster Press, 1957.

Ministry in Fiction

Bernanos, Georges. *The Diary of a Country Priest.* Macmillan Co., 1962.
Frederic, Harold. *The Damnation of Theron Ware.* Holt, Rinehart & Winston, 1960.
Greene, Graham. *The Power and the Glory.* Viking Press, 1970.
Kim, Richard E. *The Martyred.* George Braziller, 1964.
Mercer, Charles. *The Minister.* Avon Books, 1969.
Richter, Conrad. *A Simple Honorable Man.* Alfred A. Knopf, 1962.
Updike, John. *Rabbit, Run.* Fawcett, 1960.
———. *A Month of Sundays.* Fawcett, 1975.

Index